THE

CEREMONIA

CIRCLE

THE
CEREMONIAL
CIRCLE

PRACTICE, RITUAL, AND RENEWAL
FOR PERSONAL AND COMMUNITY HEALING

SEDONIA CAHILL

AND

JOSHUA HALPERN

HarperSanFrancisco
A Division of HarperCollins *Publishers*

For each tree used in the manufacture of this book's first printing, the Publisher and the Authors will arrange to plant a tree in the Central American rain forest.

Unless otherwise noted, photographs are from the collection of Sedonia Cahill and Bird Brother.

We want to thank the artists whose illustrations appear in this book. The Shell and Feather is by Dawn Wilson, the Medicine Shield is by Margie Clark, and the Dancing Woman is by Robyn Posin.

FIRST HARPERCOLLINS PAPERBACK EDITION PUBLISHED IN 1992

Library of Congress Cataloging–in–Publication Data

Cahill, Sedonia.
The ceremonial circle : practice, ritual, and renewal for personal and community healing / Sedonia Cahill & Joshua Halpern.—1st HarperCollins pbk. ed.
          p.   cm.
Includes bibliographical references.
ISBN 0–06–250154–2 (pbk. : alk. paper)
1. Ritual. 2. Circle—Religious aspects. 3. New Age movement. 4. Magic.
I. Halpern, Joshua. II. Title.
[BF1623.R6C34 1992]
291.3'8—dc20   91–55321
                                                                        CIP

93 94 95 96 RRD-H 10 9 8 7 6 5 4 3 2

This edition is printed on acid-free paper that meets the American National Standards Institute Z39.48 Standard.

TO ALL THOSE WHO DANCE IN THE CIRCLE

CONTENTS

SPEAKING FROM
THE HEART

SEDONIA'S STORY

I first stood in a spiritual circle in 1955 when I was a sophomore at Texas University. I was an unhappy student and a very out-of-place member of a prestigious social sorority. I avoided the sorority house activities as much as possible, but on this occasion we were all required to attend a country weekend retreat led by a very charismatic campus pastor. I remember almost nothing of the three-day gathering except what happened on the last afternoon. As a closure the minister spoke a few words and then asked that all of us—about fifty young women—stand and hold hands in a circle. I responded with little enthusiasm, took the hands of the two young women nearest to me, closed my eyes and half listened to the words of prayer.

My experience during the next few minutes was of such power and magnitude that it literally shaped the direction of my life. In those brief moments I no longer felt like a lost, lonely, and directionless child; instead I was a full member of a strong group, a tribe. My mind was one with the other minds; we were, in fact, one. It was not necessary to compare myself with the others and find myself lacking. There was nothing to compare as we were all one. In that circle, in that moment, we were all equal. It didn't matter who had the shiniest and curliest hair, the bluest eyes, the most graceful body, the most gorgeous wardrobe, the best grades, or even the most exciting and active social life.

Even though none of us could speak of it we had been ushered into sacred time and space. Certainly this magnetic man had been an instrument, but I am certain it was the circle that brought us into this dimension of liminality. All of my experience in those days was of isolation and extreme loneliness mixed with boredom and self-doubt. For me what had happened was a miracle of the first order.

I wish I could report that those wonderful feelings of unity and belonging had stayed with me. Instead I was left with a spiritual hunger. This longing became a prime motivator in my life.

Years later I was living in San Antonio, Texas. In those days I sometimes watched television and it was becoming increasingly difficult to ignore the faraway Eastern war that was being filmed and brought to my living room via TV. The sight of a tiny Vietnamese woman running with a look of absolute horror on her face, carrying the body of her small child burned beyond recognition, turned my dreams into nightmares. I would look at my three beautiful, happy, and healthy children and realize that if this madness didn't stop soon we would all be running and screaming in terror.

San Antonio was a military town, proud of its five military installations. The economic fabric of the town was interwoven tightly with many strings leading to the Pentagon. In this city of many thousands was a small and brave band of peaceniks, not more than twenty-five or thirty very committed individuals, all ages and colors. The children and I would join this group every Saturday afternoon in a vigil for peace in front of the Alamo. Because our numbers were small, and our cause very unpopular in those days, the group became like family. We had frequent formal meetings to discuss strategy and money raising. We all shared the staffing of a small office dedicated to draft counseling and support for soldiers who were declaring conscientious objector status, and others who were crossing borders to escape the system. We often met informally for parties, celebrations, and emotional support. In many ways we were family to one another, inspiring, consoling, and sharing.

Every Sunday morning, when others were sitting in neat church pews, we would meet in the park. We called these gatherings Agapes, after the early Christian love feasts. We would stand in a circle, sharing prayers and embraces, passing a bottle of wine and someone's homemade bread, an oddly assorted group with kids, unruly dogs, and guitars. In those days the news was so discouraging and the steps toward peace so few and so small, it was easy to feel hopeless and helpless. It was through the energy and love that was generated in these circles that we all continually renewed our commitment to the struggle.

Even as the horror show raged, haunting us all day and night, for this short hour in the circle in the park all was at peace. The world was good and beautiful, full of hope and promise. Always we left feeling renewed and ready for the struggle, knowing full well that we were part of one very large family, a global circle made of all races, colors, and creeds, and that soon the world would awaken from its delirium and join with us in the Great Love Feast of life. Though none of us probably understood it at the time, it was the circle that kept us going. For the first time in many years, I had moments of connection to others and to life.

In the late sixties I packed up my family and moved to San Francisco. We landed right in the center of the Haight Ashbury district. Days found me in the park, barefoot, happy, and in circles. Informal, spontaneous circles in the park, at the beach, at the rock concerts. Circles of dancing gypsies. Circles of shared sacraments. Circles surrounding newly emerging holy men and sages, prophets and gurus. All one big, colorful, bizarre, psychedelic swirl. Feelings and emotions that had long been repressed came to the surface and were acted out in wonderful, and sometimes strange, ways. We had no context for any of it. All we knew was that we were part of a glorious revolution and that at any moment all would be love and bliss. What glorious innocents we were!

How wonderful if all could have been so simple. The problems that I personally faced had been thirty-odd years in the making and the problems the culture faced were at least six thousand years old. Neither my problems nor the world's were going to be solved that easily or that quickly. My spiritual questing became more intense. I began to meditate, do yoga and T'ai Chi, study the tarot and I Ching, cabala and magic, macrobiotics and Tao, Sufi dancing, you name it. I went to see every holy man that came to town. I sampled everything that came my way, still searching and seeking.

Through searching and experimentation I found some of the freedom I sought for myself and my family. Still, something was missing. In the midst of all this activity, all these people, it still seemed that nothing was really happening, I wasn't really connecting with any of it. As soon as the novelty of each new experience wore off I was ready to move on.

Throughout all of this I began to make an important observation. At the big spiritual gatherings every one on the stage and at the podium was male. In the spiritual communities the leadership was always in the hands of the men. At the bookstores almost all the spiritual books were authored by men. Could this be the reason I was having difficulty relating? Perhaps it wasn't me or other women they were speaking to.

It was during this time, in the early and middle seventies, that I began to sit in circles with women. I joined a small consciousness-raising group. Most of our time and energy was spent in exploring and sharing the ways we had been used and abused, deceived and misled, undermined and misunderstood. The anger was extreme and necessary. The trick for me was to move through it and use it as a catalyst. Miraculous changes began to occur. I began to see women as beautiful sisters to be loved, trusted and enjoyed, and slowly, I began to see myself in the same way.

There were many women's gatherings in those days. Small consciousness-raising groups were meeting in living rooms all over. There were large weekend gatherings in the park for music making and teaching and playing. There was Alyssium, a wonderful drop-in center on Union Street where women could share their trials and victories, gestalt and play-act their dilemmas. And always, in all of these gatherings, the women quite naturally and easily moved into the form of a circle. Some of the time there were leaders and facilitators, but always they joined in the circle.

Slowly, out of all this sharing and focusing on problems, usually with political solutions, there began to emerge something that is being called women's spirituality. The most natural form of this spiritual democracy is the circle—the circle that is also the spiral, moving in infinite spheres into the farthest reaches of heaven and the greatest depths of the self and the earth—the circle that is beginning and ending in every moment and that has room for all those ready and willing to join the dance.

The central focus of my spiritual expression these past twelve years has been the teachings of the ancient grandmothers, and most especially the Circle Way. In 1980 I went with Steven Foster and Meredith Little to Death Valley to undertake a vision quest. The experience changed my life. Up on the mountain, in that solitary and lonely space, I learned that I really do belong here on this planet; that I, along with all of creation, have an important and beautiful thread in this exquisite tapestry that is life. There, alone on the mountain, I felt myself to be standing in a very large circle that included all that ever was created and all that ever would be. How could I ever be lonely again in such a universe!

My path has taken me again, many times, to the mountain, sometimes as a quester and more often as a vision quest guide for others. I am a creator and participant in circles. Circles of all kinds. Free and unstructured circles on the beach for each solstice and equinox. The circle of my women's lodge that meets every full moon and new moon. The circle of prayer and gratefulness that I share with those with whom I break bread. The teaching and praying circles with the vision questers in the desert. Circles with women my age who are dedicated to becoming wise elders together. Circles of explorations with others determined to understand ourselves more deeply and fully. Circles of women and men daring to speak the truth to one another. Circles of music making and dancing co-created with friends. Circles to honor birth and death, marriage and separation, coming of age and other important rites of passage. Talking staff circles with peers to resolve issues or define and refine our perceptions and values. Prayer lodge circles and all-night drumming and praying circles. Large ceremonial circles that my partner, Bird, and I lead or ones that are led by women shamans, such as the ones in this book. Circles and circles and more circles. Thus does the goddess dance with us and for us and all around us. Thus the circle grows.

The circle grew very large for me when I was part of a group of thirteen alternative healers who were invited to the Soviet Union to teach in the fall of 1990. We were in Leningrad and in the Ukraine, in Kiev we were only sixty miles from Chernobyl. As part of my work there I had the privilege of leading some very large circles. I was delighted at how quickly the people there took to the form. They loved it. It was especially sweet when we would sing songs to them in English and they would sing back their songs in Russian. There was a special poignancy in this for me, and a very deep gratitude that the cold war had thawed and we could join our voices over all the miles and the politics, that we were so much more similar than different. We left a drum, rattles, a shell, feather, and sage with a woman in each city who was interested in keeping the circle going.

I have been privileged to meet and work with many fine teachers along the way these past years. Women who are calling and leading circles. Women whose commitment is deep and whose visions are strong. Writing this book is a way for me to acknowledge some of the people who have been important to my work. In writing this book we are weaving yet another circle.

I wish to honor all that has brought me to this moment. So much has given away to me, all the plants and animals that have given that I might have food and clothing and housing, all the hands and hearts that have supported and nourished me on the way, all those who have taught me difficult teachings as well as those whose teachings have been joyful and ecstatic.

I give special thanks to the women of the Owl/Eagle Lodge who have taught me so much about good-natured sweetness and sisterhood, and the sharing of power; to the women in the Spider Lodge who teach me about being authentic and caring for all the parts of the inner family; to the women and men in the Heart Lodge who encourage the best in me always; to all the members of the other circles and lodges I belong to who help and inspire me on my Medicine journey; to the courageous and beautiful vision questers who come from all parts of the world and who, each and every one, dance in my heart; to my Cherokee elder, Grandpa Roberts, who knew more about unconditional love than anyone I have ever known; to Harley Swiftdeer for his beautiful and inspiring Medicine Wheel teachings; to Steven Foster and Meredith Little who first took me to the mountain; to Grandmother Evelyn Eaton for her gracious way of walking her elderhood; to my editor and friend, Michael Toms, for believing in me and my work; to my spirit-sister, Jana, who used to place little magical gifts in a secret place near the computer to encourage me to get on it and write; to my three children, Brad, Gray, and Annie Laurie, of each of whom I am very proud; to my most beloved partner, Bird, who has listened to my excitement and despair about the project, has nurtured and encouraged me; to my primary teacher, the desert wind, of whom I am an apprentice and who speaks to me so strongly and constantly, and most especially I dedicate this book to all of you who are willing to "walk your talk" and put your life on the line to bring this beautiful earth jewel into balance and harmony.

Joshua's story

I have lived in the coastal redwoods for most of my life. As a young man I followed deer trails in the shadowy vestiges of the holy, ancient redwood rain forest. It was the first time that light hit the earth in thousands of years. I felt the ghosts of Miwoks and Pomos. The land was soaked in blood. Genocide decimated the tribes and the trees, but not even genocide could stop the spirit that was reborn in the night. The owl became the guardian of the land. Tukku'uli.

I met an old shaman who lived nearby. He made a fire circle and blew on the trumpet of the earth. He spoke through the spirit world. He taught me that the rain was more than tears—called by singing the morning star song.

What happened to me was that the Indian spirit merged and resonated with the fire in my own bones. Jewish Tribal Bones, bones that had also been through genocide. I faced my own past, mirrors, dharma.

My mother was born in Romania. I was born in Berkeley. My parents were radicals. I went to public school, and for the first years of my life I lived in the poor part of town. Living in the ghetto might have been a solidarity gesture to the working class for my parents, but for me it was reality. I identified with blacks more than whites. I experienced my first spiritual awakening in a black Baptist church. I walked in both worlds. I was breast-fed by a black woman while my mother taught black kids how to read.

While I was in tenth grade I left home to attend a Quaker boarding school in the Sierra Nevadas. I made myself a teepee out in the woods and spent every chance I had by the creek. I developed concern for community and group process and made a commitment to living on the earth. I knew in my gut that I wanted to live on the land.

On my first road trip after leaving school, I went out looking for a place to live. I was sixteen. I went south on U.S. Highway 1 and made it to Big Sur in one day. The first night out I slept in the woods alone. The second night I experienced my first powerful, spiritual circle and was introduced to the drum. Big Sur, I later learned, was the place on the Pacific Coast where white men kept the black drum alive. When I heard the drums wailing, my bones woke up. "The ghost," as Black Elk called it, came alive.

I got my first drum and lived for seven years without electricity or running water, catching the rain, gathering seaweed with the tides, studying natural medicine.

I drummed through the seasons in one place for many years. I worked a homestead. My son was born on the cabin floor.

In 1976 I began to participate in structured circles and learned much from Robert Greenway, a wise elder poet with whom I and a group of twenty others spent a month-long period in the wilderness near Albion, California. Our purpose was to experience the "periodicities" of nature by revolving daily life around the circle; sleeping in circle, eating in circle, sweating, staying up all night in circle. I was introduced to many of the techniques of circle council with him. I also wish to thank Robert Hall, M.D., with whom I circled for a month in the city, barely going outside the perimeter of a gestalt group. Both pushed me forward in my circle work.

In 1980 I wrote a book with my dad and in the process realized I had men's work to do. I set out to investigate the male psyche. I developed a burning desire to see exactly what the male psyche *was*. Was there anything intrinsic in what I now refer to as "male terror"? I wanted to see what boys came in with and what was laid on them from conditioning.

I began drumming for a group of midwives at Artemis College in Occidental, California. I did this for two years. From the experience of going to births and witnessing the process of incarnation, I wrote *Visions of the New Family*. I was deeply impressed with the integrity of energy I found among the midwives. They were very receptive to the drum. The director of the school, Nan Kohler, is a traditional birth attendant and she consciously moves her students toward a deeper awareness of the birth process.

Drumming and birthing go together. People become fertile when they drum. It dawned on me how profound the shared resonance of the ceremonial circle was. We met regularly every Friday and four times a year for a day and night of circle songs. Every Friday we came in from our busy lives, slowed down, evoked the spirit, and made a circle. In the midst of what seemed like an inordinate amount of chaos, children squawking and murmuring at the breast, the circle was called, evoked, formed.

In this rigorous context it was hard to maintain a ceremonial pulse. There were many distractions, yet we learned to focus and to bring the sacred into the chaos. I very much appreciated the energy of this circle, for it was not removed from reality. As we circled and sang and prayed and evoked I came to realize that we were offering the kindest present we could give to our children: a way to make a viable culture.

After completing a two-year apprenticeship, it became clear to me that the next step in my exploration was to begin to develop the circle process in the wider community. I did this by establishing my men's drumming lodge and going out on the road to sit in circle with many kinds of people, engaging in many different kinds of practices.

I strongly encourage both men and women to form drumming circles with their own kind. The best way I know to drum and circle is sometimes with those of your own gender but most of the time with everyone.

I have been in a tight knit though kindly open drumming circle with a group of men for over ten years. We started drumming together when some of them were in their early teens. We have grown up together. They have witnessed me become a father. I have been there as they came down from the mountain. We have gone together as a troupe to healing festivals. We had a chance to drum for Robert Bly and afterward he came up to my place for the night and told me to claim a thousand hours with my dad: I have been consciously trying to do this. I flail and fall but still I am committed to this work on a level that is in my blood.

The circle is for us all. It is like the drum: It is round and contains everything. While it is poetic for the circle to be referred to as a feminine form, it is no more feminine than water or earth, nor is it any more a woman's tool than the drum is a man's.

The real purpose of circle work is to help in the process of forming community. For me that begins at home and extends outward. That is the real, challenging path and why it is essential that we learn from each other and share what we know.

I learn about circling from many places. One important circle for me has been a public interracial, urban, drumming scene in Biko Plaza on the University of California's Berkeley campus. This circle happens on Sunday afternoons, and has for decades, with many of the same drummers, some of whom were buddies of mine from grade school. The circle is open, public, available. There are better days and worse days but the quality of sound that comes from the participants is consistently shamanic.

I learn about circling and drumming from the ghost dancers and ceremonialists who travel the Rainbow Gypsy Trail on the Pacific Northwest summer dance route. There is now an actual route, and a great spiritual renewal is happening in the midst of the destruction. The renewal culture has developed its own unique shamans and some of them have been praying and making circles for twenty-five years.

Mostly I learn by chopping wood and carrying water. I have never been able to get away with anything. My practice pertains to my daily life. I think wholeness is hauntingly simple and that it occurs naturally when we are conscious. We all contain the Shekinah. We are all embodiments of a Holy Spirit. We are all One in the Soul.

The challenge before us is to find our own circles. Each of us has to find our own life companions, right here, right now. All of us need friends with whom to build community. I think this is especially so for those of us involved in the raising of children. The challenge is to build a viable extended family and in the process build schools, holistic health clinics, organic farms. Viable, sustainable communities are our most potent survival tool. The circle is a profound resource for building community.

It is easy to know principles, but to learn them they must be lived. The forming of groups can be difficult and dangerous. People need the ballast of the earth, and this is provided by the circular form. To survive the coming changes to which our earth is heir we have to join together.

Acknowledgments: Dr. Donald Solomon, the Faist and Charlot families, David Peri, Gabrielle Roth, Brandt Segunda, Inti, Lillian Marsola, Karen Ray, Al Locatelli, Manu, Ethan, Josh, Janet Lederman, my neighbors on Joy Ridge, my sister Tova, and especially Sarah Tiferet and Elijah David.

Obeisance to: Black Elk, Babatunde Olatunji, Murshid Mackie, and Meher Baba.

THE
CEREMONIAL
CIRCLE

CALL TO THE CIRCLE

*Everything the power of the world does is
done in a circle.*
BLACK ELK, from *Black Elk Speaks*

It has been hot for a week, the fog has come in during the night, and water now drips from the boughs of the trees. The squash blossoms are opening as the sun comes through. People are beginning to stir in their houses, from a backyard a baby's cry for food can be heard, a woman watches television, the meteorologist points to satellite pictures of an oncoming weather system; an older man who has recently had a heart attack starts out on his morning walk.

The day is beginning all over the spinning earth as our lives are ordered by a circular, returning pattern of light and darkness. In New Mexico an old Indian woman goes outside her house and looks to the East, the home of the sun; in Jerusalem an old Jew ties up his phylacteries; householders and sadhus bathe in the Ganges; children everywhere long to go out-of-doors and greet the sun. There are over five billion of us now on this little planet, separate yet essentially the same, all born from the body of woman, dependent upon the earth for seed and sustenance.

We all greet the same sun from the same ground of the same spinning earth and all breathe the same air, yet there is little harmony on this earth. We are divided. Even those who believe in the same god kill one another. Political solutions without spirit seem futile, and yet the sun still returns each day, kissing the night good-bye, bringing and ending the dawn, greeting all with the benediction of light.

There is beauty and destruction. The fire that was to precede the sign

1

of the rainbow is still raging and yet the rainbow is clearly visible through the tears. If we could strip away the ideologies that separate us, stop the greedy destruction, and meet by the riverside, we would discover that we are all children of the same earth and that our lives are patterned by the ceremonial flow of the sun, moon, seasons, and tides. We are all one in the spirit and in the body.

It is this inner gnosis and experience of oneness that is at the heart of all spiritual traditions, the cosmic stream that we originate from. All paths of heart make known that we are one, that there is one earth, that all roads lead to the one sun. All our bones will turn to ash and mineral, as life and death spin their ancient weave. All the demarcations on all the maps are meaningless now, we are a one-earth people. The whole planet has been interconnected. We are a whole system and are beginning to understand that we cannot deceive nature.

The purpose of ceremony is to bring an awareness of such unity into consciousness. It is a necessary component of the human learning process, yet now it must be relearned. When people lived closer to the earth, when each community had to provide its own food, ceremony was an integral part of life. There was always a big dance on corn-planting day. Though we have advanced scientifically we have forgotten how to maintain a sustainable and viable culture. Typical corn seeds in typical seed shops are hybrid mutants that hold little food value except starch and sugar and are very susceptible to disease. We are in somewhat the same dilemma as the seeds. Shut off from nature, most of us live in cities that may have been built to protect but now hold their inhabitants hostage.

The original methods of natural worship and devotion, which so many tribal people took for granted and which healed them, such as dancing and singing in a circle, have been secularized. The altar was raised high above the ground and became dominated by a male-centric way of viewing god and life.

A well-functioning ceremonial circle mitigates duality and can help heal the dichotomy between spirit and matter. It can open up a world of self-discovery and create a place where the concerns of the genders are the same, where both recognize their responsibility to the earth as partners, parents, and citizens. One of the great opportunities the circle provides is a space to collaborate as creative women and men. We are in the process of returning to a circular form of communion because it works.

The circle is a form that arises from nature's breath and imprints upon the culture as well as our individual cells. Each component of our body is a miniature solar system, spinning in a circular motion. There is a song that goes, "I am a circle I am healing you, You are a circle, You are healing me," which carries a biological as well as a spiritual truth.

When people gather in a circle and their intentions are aligned it can help them drop the armoring of their personality structures. When you are struggling with an addiction, and you meet with others in a circle to discuss and feel your issues, with others as witness, it heals something inside. On the societal level it is also healing because it is a perfect form for joining different groupings of people.

The circle contains a magical power that defies superficial boundaries. If we want to bring peace between the races it is important to meet in small, interracial circles; to bring peace between women and men we must create truthful circles containing both.

Ceremonial circling best expresses the egalitarian principles upon which the essence of all spiritual experience is based. The circle form of ceremony is very simple. It is available to all of us regardless of our backgrounds or experiences, though there are many ancient tools that can be used to make the process more effective.

The shamanic tools shared in this book, like all tools, must be used with clear intention for good to result. Many shamanic-circle techniques amplify energy and unveil the illusions that cloud our lives. They are powerful and must be used with a concern for the good of all life, the total earth. The roots of shamanism have grown out of the circle, are ancient, and should be used with respect as tools for creation. If you honor them you will become a responsible co-creator of the entire tribe's welfare, of the health and harmony of the earth. To defend the earth we must all become translators of dreams and makers of magic through the creation of ceremonial circles.

The circle form can be used very effectively in many settings, lending a tone that was not there before. It can be used in a study group, an anti-nuke group, a women's health collective, at the volunteer fire department meetings. Practice it as often as you can because circling brings life to a meeting and every group can benefit from a ceremonial focus. Circles make whatever is happening more conscious.

The process of ceremony, with or without ritual, introduces into a meeting a depth of feeling that transcends the business at hand. It's been our experience that sometimes people will begin to cry the first time they sit in a circle. At one circle a woman began to sob quietly after we had been rattling and drumming for a few minutes. She later said that she had heard those sounds and felt those feelings in her solitude for a long time and didn't know she could have the longing satisfied. The circle awakened a primal memory in her. Her hunger was deep and real and her tears were tears of gratitude.

Once you have been in a conscious circle with someone a bond is created that will last even if you only see each other infrequently. However, if you circle with someone often you will begin to feel a part of the same tribe. This is the most socially potent result of circling. Being a part of a group of people, an extended family, enriches life in many ways. The isolation attendant to the nuclear family is replaced with a feeling of communion. The capacity to process what one is feeling and clear the way for the new is enhanced. A new kind of spiritual/political power can be generated. This factor, still largely known only in its potential, is one of the aspects of circling that holds the most exciting possibilities.

Once a circle is formed and happening it is natural to begin to reach out and join with other circles. Each circle can be thought of as a "cell of the Goddess," joined with other circles/cells to recreate the body of renewed humanity. This, after all, is what must happen for our species to survive. The limits of tribal identification must be expanded to include everyone, for everyone is a child of the same earth, circle, and nation. The only way such feelings of inclusiveness can rise from the realm of utopian speculation to actualization is by gathering in small groups, getting organized, and then expanding in consciousness to include all, in other words to act locally and think globally.

Before we can actualize the global healing potential of the circle, we must integrate circling into our daily lives. This is where the real challenge is and why we have focused on practical ways of doing this as well as sharing stories of ways it has been done. One of the functions of an ongoing circle can be to reach out and help others get circles going. We have included guidelines for doing this. Still, even with all this information, the work of getting oneself into a circle can be very difficult and lonely. In the beginning one may not succeed. We have talked to people who have tried and have not been able to get a circle going, but even if it takes you a while, the effort is worth it. Every attempt to circle sets into motion a healing energy and even if this healing energy is not realized in the way you would like, it does not mean there has been no positive effect. We guarantee that if you persevere you will find a community with which to circle.

Part of the function of this book is to connect people with circles and help you in your circling endeavors. We have spoken to many active people who are working with the healing potential of circles and more and more people are being called to this work. Even if you have to travel a distance to participate in circles, when you find one it will enhance your life. In this instance established circles in other areas can provide a basis for creating your spiritual community. Circling has such a strong bonding effect that a community can be established even if the members live hundreds of miles apart. It is very feasible to plan one's year so that vacations and holidays are spent with a circling community.

Of course, the optimal situation is to have a ceremonial community where you live, but it is not necessary in order to experience the benefits of being a part of one. We are a global community and, be it in one's neighborhood or extended across the landscape, it is central to the purpose of this book that each of us feel a part of something larger.

It is our intention in sharing the technology of circling and the experiences of those who are doing it that you become empowered to start one of your own, or to integrate circling into an already functioning group. If you are willing to work, to gather with others, the tools provided in this book and the circle form of ceremony will assist you in building a sustainable culture.

ONE

RECLAIMING THE SACRED

The shaman speaks for wild animals, the spirits of plants, the spirits of
mountains, of watersheds. He or she sings for them.
GARY SNYDER

SHAMANISM AND CULTURE

Culture comes up out of the earth, vibrating through the body, as each individual affirms life and expresses her or his unique creativity. It is kept alive by consciously honoring the sacredness of the four Great Mysteries: food, sex, birth, and death. The ceremonial arts are channels for people to express their relationship with these primal mysteries.

Culture is not synonymous with society, it is the friendly bacteria of society. It thrives when there is a web of interrelatedness between the individual and community, and between the community and nature. Culture prospers when the work that each member performs is in alignment with the earth and is a direct and sacred expression of Spirit. A healthy culture is one that lives within the fundamental laws of reciprocity, where no more is taken than will be returned.

Civilization is merciless and brutal to nature and culture because it is so out of balance with the Sacred Laws. It has taken the holiness of birth and twisted it into a clinical exercise; death is feared; sex is demeaned and trivialized; food is denatured and toxic. Collectively we are faced with the challenge of building a sustainable, renewable culture. Our work is to reclaim the sacred dimension and bring it into relationship to the mysteries.

The ceremonial circle is the most effective form for breathing new life into the soul and spirit of human interchange, for inspiring renewed personal vision and for recreating a cohesive community. The circle allows the individual to feel part of a larger being that has a life of its own and whose power is solely available to nurture. The connection between people in a ceremonial circle creates the threads that will weave the human species back into the Sacred Hoop of Life.

Inside our cells we each hold an archive of memory from a time when the sacred mysteries were approached with awe and reverence. In our ancestral past we have all been part of a cohesive culture where communal life was in tune with the ecosystem, where the family was part of community and not an isolated unit, where there wasn't a dichotomy between ecology and theology, where life, with all its joys and sorrows, was celebrated in ceremonial gatherings.

The current revival of the shamanic arts and the ceremonial circle is a response to the heart's longing to return to a harmonic vibration with the earth. The shaman's function has traditionally been to serve the community by evoking sacred powers. Shamanic practice involves looking straight into the heart of tonal, worldly reality, no matter how disturbing. A shaman is able to access information from travels into non-ordinary states of being and return with knowledge that will assist in healing.

Shamanic practice grows from need. In tribal cultures there were enough shamans so that if someone had a dream that utilized water images to reveal the psyche's content, he or she was sent to a shaman who knew how to work with that element. Shamanism is undergoing a period of revival and redefinition as it becomes part of modern life. It is our contention that every time someone moves from fragmentation and isolation into unity, it is an initiation ever as rigorous as preindustrial shamans had to go through.

In either case there is a wounding and a healing that is the shamanic paradigm. Children who have lived in a divorced family and put back together their psyches so they could love both themselves and their parents have been initiated into shamanic practice. This process of dis-memberment and re-membering is the criteria for healing.

Shamans are technicians of the sacred, and nothing is more sacred than the actual processes of life. The need for deeper, shamanic help is part of human reality, but it is important for us not to mystify the function of the shaman. Every time a mother is actively involved in the birth of her child it is a shamanic initiation for the mother. When a daughter is able to share and celebrate with her mother the experience of becoming a woman it is a shamanic initiation into the mystery of sex for both of them. Whenever the need for nurturance is acknowledged there is a resurgence in shamanic practice.

The people in northern California who hug old-growth redwoods as the bulldozers and chain saws are roaring in their ears are functioning as cultural shamans. Everybody who ever wrote a poem that cried out for peace or who spoke clearly about what they needed, or who loves the shape of laughter, or has reached out to welcome others into the circle, holds a piece of the revival of cultrual shamanism. Wherever people are reinhabiting the earth and living in ecological sanity there is a resurgence in shamanic practice.

Elizabeth Cogburn tells us that there are two types of students of shamanism, the Black-Painted Face and the Red-Painted Face. The Black-Painted Face is one who has done a long apprenticeship with a respected teacher. She or he learns that there are very precise and traditional ways of being a shaman. The downfall of this approach is that it is often accompanied by a need to criticize those who have not had the same teacher or training. This method is usually controlled, direct, and piercing.

The Red-Painted Face studies with many teachers along the way, but most of his or her guidance comes from the place deep inside that knows when things are right and appropriate, and from their intimate relationships with friends, family, lovers, and nature. This method is spontaneous, the energy flowing and undulating and the mode inclusive.

The shamanism of cultural renewal requires many new forms to respond to the world as it is now. Since we live in a multicultural society that is the repository of many traditional teachings and ceremonial methods, our circles will necessarily reflect many influences.

There is an ongoing discussion between some Native Americans and people who are searching for an earth-centered spiritual path about the propriety of sharing ceremonial ways with white people. We honor the feeling among some that their ancient ways are being trivialized and exploited. There have been misuses of sacred teachings. This happens with everything; there are people who have misused yoga and the I Ching and every other teaching that has found its way into contemporary life.

We are a fragmented people searching for a way that can bring meaning and depth and healing to our lives, but there is no holding back the wisdom of this earth. Everyone born on this earth's soil is a native person now and must learn to live in harmony and balance.

Although we wish that time could be rolled back and the stewardship of Turtle Island, a Native American name for North America, restored to the original inhabitants, such will never happen. There is no going back to anything. We are a rainbow people now and we must walk a rainbow path that is woven from the strands of all the wisdom teachings. We have no choice but to go forward into the unknown and we must try to do it

Women and men dance around a Sun Dance pole. *Photo: Elizabeth Cogburn*

with dignity and respect, being sensitive to the cultural identity and heritage of the people we are learning from. The transmission of useful shamanic knowledge is the real issue.

Every earth-based culture has had a tradition of shamanism, such as the old Chinese Taoists, Irish Druids, Siberians, Poles, English bards, East Indian Shivites, Persian Zoroastrians, and Japanese Shintos. Since the cultural blossoming and the back-to-the-earth movement of the sixties there has been an interest in these traditions that was not academic, but that came from a spiritual yearning. That yearning has created the soil, and the seeds have been planted for a shamanic revival that is appropriate to this time and place.

There have been many transmissions of sacred shamanic knowledge, some of which can only take place with a living teacher with whom one has direct, daily contact, so that the teacher can observe the daily patterns, inclinations, and tendencies of the student. Finding an authentic shamanic teacher, one who can really bring you into this deeper level, not just talk about it, is a very special blessing that the circle process does not supersede.

Since the decimation of tribal village life the transmission of sacred knowledge has had to rely upon new methods. The foremost among them is the circle-making process whereby people gather consciously in a ceremonial way with the goal of forging a link with an essential oneness that is at the core of all teaching.

THE CIRCLE AS A SACRED FORM FOR CEREMONY

Though we may bring knowledge from various traditions into a circle, the circle itself, if it is vital, will produce its own healing and shamanic message that is exactly appropriate for this time and place. It is better to gather within the protection of a circle of friends and find one's own way rather than try spiritual systems that are divorced from present-time reality.

Another signature of authentic shamanic practice is that it is part of the consciousness that arises from a cohesive community. Each group of people making ceremonial circles in their bio-region develops its own unique shamanistic forms. While it is interesting, and sometimes beneficial, to study shamanic practices from around the globe, unless shamanism emerges from the place where we live and the circles we are involved in, it will not be vital. It is possible to take on the trappings and sing the songs and look the part and still the practice will not be relevant.

Authentic shamanic practice stems from a circle of people who are involved in where they live, who feel part of their bio-region, who know the ways of the moon, whose diets are attuned to the seasons. Authentic shamanic practice is in service to the personal, and responsive to the political realities that affect life.

In a very palpable way people all over the earth are awakening to their oneness; everybody who ever knitted one or various strands together in the weaving has functioned in a shamanistic way and been part of the healing and renewal. The challenge is to maintain a positive attitude and not succumb to psychic numbing while facing the global crisis. In this way we are able to empower ourselves and provide what we need for our daily lives in a way that is harmonious with the ecological reality of our bio-system. An essential part of cultural shamanism and the circle-making process is to create a viable community and from the strength of it begin to potently respond to the beauty of the larger world as well as to the distress.

Shamanic practice that informs the daily life activities of a community is crucial to the development of a renewing culture. It is necessary to develop ceremonies that enrich all the aspects of our life, that reveal all the faces of the divine. Ceremony knits the divine back to the living tree, draws inspiration into the temple of the body. To be successful in life, to have an abundance to share with your friends and family, it is necessary to acknowledge the sacredness of the ground and the magic of all the transformations of life; from sperm and egg into a living creature in the blisswaters of the womb; from seed to plant; from wounded one to healing one; from body to body.

ISSUES OF POWER AND THE SHARING OF SHAMANIC TOOLS

Our wise ancestors knew about the ways of the ground, they knew that the corn could not truly nourish unless it was planted with prayer. It may grow physically, it may even be harvested, sold, and consumed, but it will not nurture the cells of the living, spirit-filled body unless it is sown with reverence. The ancient ceremonial dances had their genesis in birthing and planting and observing the cyclic flow of the seasons.

The ceremonial circles that occur in a viable community become entities, they hold a shamanic force and take on a presence of their own as they bridge the breaks in the line and curve the corners of the plane so that there can be room for us all. The circle extends the perimeter, not by dissolving it but by solidifying it, so the self is connected to a deeper level, the place where joining and individuality exist in collaboration, allowed to pursue conjointly the end they both share.

The value of learning how to circle in a ceremonial way, utilizing ancient shamanic tools such as prayer and invoking, the talking stick and the drum, is in its potency to bring people together. The circle is the perfect form for cultural renewal because each circle symbolically represents the whole of humanity and is a microcosm of a harmonious potential.

TAKING RESPONSIBILITY FOR THE EARTH AND COMMUNITY

Healing happens when we learn to attune to the primal energies of the earth. Then and only then will the potential of technology be realized. Right now we are linked up in the technological grid but not yet in a place to respond to the information. We have been physically interconnected by technology but not spiritually. We utilize Aquarian energy to talk on the phone and monitor networks of planetary news, allowing us to see the global destruction in dying color, but we haven't yet realized the responsi-

Large ceremonial circle at a Gaia Reborn festival sponsored by Motherpeace Institute in San Francisco. *Photo: Vicki Noble*

bility inherent in that viewing. Government is lagging light years behind in responding to the ecological crisis. The disaster at Chernobyl showed us just how ridiculous borderlines are. The nuclear cloud does not wait at the border to have its visa stamped.

The time has come, the need is extreme, each of us has to come forward from our own circle of power and break down the borderlines. Each of us can call forth the shaman within. We all have the power to call a circle, to transform, to heal the terrible predicament we are all in. Trust yourself. As long as your heart is pure, you will create good.

TWO

WEAVING THE BASKET

. . . for everything that lives is Holy.
WILLIAM BLAKE

To initiate or participate in a ceremonial circle requires a clear intention and a degree of personal power, resolve, and endurance. Just to claim the space in which to circle requires the ability to step out of world time and move into sacred time, and to find sacred time in a society that is ordered by hierarchy requires a reorientation of values, from consumerism to spirit, from audience to participation. It requires the ability to communicate intention and share vision; it requires a strong commitment. A circle is held together by the clear and strong intentions of the participants.

Ceremony requires respect, which is the gateway to entering sacred time and space. To be in sacred time and space is to be totally in present time. It is to know oneself as part of a vast circle in which all expressions of life, the birds, animals, trees, insects, rocks are our brothers and sisters, all equally beloved and vital to the Great Mother.

When we make ceremonial circles we create a form in which to align ourselves with the sacred pulse of life. To form a circle establishes the possibility for communion. Whether or not that possibility is realized depends on how well the participants can work with the energy. Forming a ceremony is like setting out a mound of clay before a sculptor. The initial impulse to create a work of art is beautiful and pure but is not enough. So too with the circle.

One learns to create and participate in ceremonial circles by being a part of them. We have been involved in circle making for many years. We have met and studied with traditional ceremonialists and people, mostly women, who are creating their own circle forms. We have drawn from this body of experience, as well as our own work, to create this book.

Everyone who gets involved in ceremonial work will learn unique lessons. Every time and place in which a ceremonial circle is formed is a new experience and adds to the body of knowledge of all circlers. Many influences, subtle and gross, affect the experience of the circle. Some of them can be anticipated, others spring mysteriously from the unique gestalt of the moment.

The following guidelines and considerations are just that, suggestions and observations. Some will be valid for you and some won't. There is no one way to form a ceremonial circle. You will constantly learn new ways, which is what makes this a dynamic and exciting form.

Making sacred space is an intricate process which requires that each participant get clear about their motivations. That a space is made sacred does not mean that the human struggle involved in having an ego will disappear, merely that it is a safe space in which to work on one's self. The energy of a circle can create a space that can allow for the unorthodox to enter and the unexpected to happen.

Every moment and every thing is an expression of Spirit; all of life is sacred. But our lives are so full and busy that we often lose sight of this. We designate a certain time of the week or of the year as sacred time and certain places, such as cathedrals or temples or special groves of trees, as sacred space, forgetting that every piece of ground that we stand on is sacred ground. Sitting in a circle and taking the time to deeply connect with those in the circle can bring us back into the awareness of the sacred. It really is a matter of taking the time to connect. Once we do, we become deeply aware of the uniqueness and sacredness of every thing around us, and within us as well.

Sacred time and space is not otherworldly, though it cannot be measured by this world, by the known. One of the primary purposes of circling is to bring sacredness into daily life. When the Hopis plant their corn they are in sacred time and space. Though planting is a practical act, necessary to survival, it is turned into a sacred act through intention and discipline. Unlike many of the Eastern models of religious experience, which promote a transcendental approach to the sacred, the sacredness of which we speak is earthly, a primal glory. The root derivation of the word glory means to rise. Primal glory comes from the earth, from the heart, from the blood.

The internal experience of being in sacred time and space is a feeling of timelessness, in which only the here and now exists, a focus on what is happening both inside and outside of yourself, and can include an absolute knowing that you are related to all living creatures, a feeling of awe for the beauty of life. Most of us can remember, if we reflect on it, many moments in our childhood when all these feelings were present. Perhaps they came while sitting alone high up in your favorite tree watching the dazzling light playing through the branches; perhaps while walking alone or with your best friend down by the creek bed, listening to the music of the water.

The urge for the sacred is innate. The work of the adult is to bring sacredness into one's life in a conscious way and in a way that involves others. If everybody goes off by themselves to experience the sacred, or experience it only in prescribed places, ways, and times, the culture can and will deteriorate. Though it is essential for spiritual maturation that the individual be able to be alone and complete, it is also essential for cultural regeneration and for the protection of the earth that we be able to gather together to experience sacredness, that we bring our family and friends with us, that we make new friends in the circle.

Making Sacred Time and Space

Several years ago I, Sedonia, led a circle for nine women at a growth center in California. As usual, we began the circle with a combination of drumming, rattling, and singing, which are my favorite tools to move through the threshold into sacred time and space. I was both surprised and pleased at how quickly these women were able to freely use their voices to express deep emotions. Though they were all new to this free-form vocalizing, which relies on sounds rather than words, all but one of them were able to be both playful and powerful.

After the music had taken us to the deep place where we needed to be, we began to sit in council and the women were invited to share something from their hearts that we could all speak to. I have found that the sharing of real feeling in the context of the circle/council touches a radically authentic place within us. It certainly did this time.

One of the women introduced a question to the council. She said that she had been experiencing a great deal of fear and anxiety and wanted to know how to reconcile her spiritual life with her work. Her work was not nourishing, but she was afraid to give up the security. Her anxiety about the world situation was also amplifying her personal fears about her future. The circle provided a perfect container for us to explore the dilemma of the dichotomy that she felt between her inner life and the world.

We all could identify with her fear. After we each had spoken our truth we decided to explore the fear more deeply. I began a slow, quiet drum beat and asked her to tell/chant her fears. She began, "I won't have food," and the group responded, "She is hungry, She will starve." Then she said, "I won't have a home." We replied, "She has no place to sleep, She has no place to live." "I won't have any money. I can't get what I need." "She has no money. She can't get what she needs." "No one will help me, I will get sick." "She'll get sick and no one will help her." "I am dying." "She is dying." "No one will help me, Nobody loves me, Nobody cares." "Nobody loves her, nobody cares." "I will die." "She will die." "Death." "Death." "Death." "Death." Her words and our responses were totally spontaneous.

I asked her if she could dance with Death and she began to move with the rhythm of our chanting and the drum. She danced until it exhausted her, then lay facedown in the center of the circle. She lay there in silence for a few moments, still deeply into her process, as we held the silent healing space for her. The tribal feeling of support, acceptance, and shared experience, which the circle provides, allowed for catharsis, not only for the spokeswoman of fear, but for all those who could surrender to the healing.

However, as often happens, one woman was intimidated by fear of her own shadow. She was the same woman who was not able to join in the chanting earlier. While the first woman was on the floor after her dance, she moved in, commanded her to turn over, placed a lit candle at her head and began to do a "healing" on her. Like so many who are frightened of their own inner shadow places, she wanted to introduce the "light" before the moment was ripe. Her response to fear was not honest and direct. Whereas one woman was able to bring her fear into the group in an inquiring and authentic manner, by stating her needs clearly and vulnerably to the group, another brought her fear into the group in a manipulative way.

Her reaction is typical of some people who are attracted to circling but who do not trust the innate healing quality that emerges from the process. There are many people who want only to focus on the good, bright, cheery side of the road, but the road we are on must be cleansed by tears. There have been too many lies. To live a life of authenticity requires the courage to face the totality of being, not just the sweetness. The confusing result upon the circle when someone tries to "save" is that it strikes a responsive chord in most people. We all have that place inside that does not want to go through the process of opening, that just wants to be open. The sacred time and space of the circle facilitates opening but it cannot do away with the process that precedes opening. A flower does not just open to the sun; there is a gestation period before it can receive the light.

I felt uncomfortable with her intervention but I sat and watched the process. I was certain that the psychodrama had ended sooner than it really needed and that no one needed to do a "healing" on the woman in the center, that as a group we had all participated in a healing process, but I was also aware that the woman on the floor was all right, in spite of the intervention. I don't always do it this way. At some other time I might feel it appropriate to deal with the fear motive of an intervening person, but in this instance it didn't seem necessary.

Exercise for Experiencing the Sacred

There are many ancient techniques to enter into deeper and higher states of consciousness. Here is one that you might like to experience:

Find a friend, a quiet place, and a rattle. If you do not have a rattle, you can use an empty vitamin bottle and put in some uncooked beans or pebbles.

There is a variation in posture depending on whether you are a man or a woman. A woman sits during the exercise and a man stands. Now place your right hand, open-palmed, on your heart and your left hand about an inch below your navel. Close your eyes, relax, and have a friend rattle in a steady, even pulse for seven minutes.

This exercise opens up the channels to archaic experience, to the original primal sacredness that exists within you all the time. We know an art therapist who utilizes this exercise to access creative inspiration. It can be a helpful tool for facilitating communication, centering, and sharing.

STRUCTURE OF THE CIRCLE

Though containing an intrinsic form, the activities of a circle can range from anarchic to highly ordered depending upon the intention of the participants. If the conveners of circles have a specific form in mind, it is up to them to communicate their intention and inquire whether the group agrees with their vision. There are also times when a convener will call a circle and allow a spontaneous and improvised happening to occur. Such considerations will depend upon whether the participants have a cohesiveness or whether they are coming from different places; whether the group includes children; whether a specific issue is being grappled with; and whether the purpose of the circle is purely celebratory.

After living in one place for a number of years I, Joshua, decided to reach out to the larger community by establishing a circle that celebrated the solstices and equinoxes. I chose to hold the circles at a local beach and open them to anyone who wanted to attend. I put a notice in the local alternative community calendar and placed announcements at various food and book stores around the county. In doing it this way I knew that the circle would have to be flexible and spontaneous and able to handle the energy of children. I made a commitment to these seasonal circles for five years and except for the winter solstice, when the weather made it unfeasible to be outdoors, I was there at each turn of the yearly cycle.

I would get to the beach early and pick a spot, often making a circle out of seaweed and driftwood. I brought rainbow flags to tie on sticks around the circle, drums, rattles, and water, and waited for people to arrive. Each season and each year the circles were different. When the weather was very beautiful fifty people might attend. At times when it was foggy there might be only a handful of people.

I especially liked the fact that the circle was held on a public beach where many people who had never seen a circle would have the chance to witness and perhaps even join in. People on the beach were very curious and often asked what cult we belonged to and it was always gratifying to be able to tell them that we were just folks from all different walks of life celebrating the turning of the sun.

The looseness of the circle permitted many people to participate but also had other repercussions. One drawback to the unstructured form was that once I stopped convening the circles they ceased to happen. On the other hand, I wanted people who would not normally circle to have the chance and in this respect it was a success.

We both come from the countercultural movement of the sixties and were a part of the revolution against structure of any type. Everything was to be free and spontaneous and happen from the moment. There was wisdom and beauty in this and some wonderful things happened. However there was so much that could have grown out of all that creativity and enthusiasm that didn't because of the absence of structure. Much good did happen in those exciting years, but these are different times. The flower children have grown up, we have lost most of our naiveté, we have learned that to make things happen and to bring about positive social change we need to create and use structure in appropriate ways. Structure can be vital when it is used in ways that cradle and contain energy rather than restrict it. The structure provides a container in which much can happen that is free and unexpected.

The circle has an inherent energy current of its own but how this current is tapped into involves psychological processes. We have come to appreciate a circle that has a well-defined structure because it can make a safe and supporting place for the unexpected. We have often experienced that in circles that don't have structure the energy tends to become chaotic and dissipates into nothing, whereas in structured circles there is room for chaos but also the tools and intention to bring the energy back into focus when the time is right.

When you call a circle certain responsibilities having to do with structure are involved. The balance between structure and nonstructure is very delicate, and to be the one in charge requires a great deal of sensitivity and awareness. Too much direction can stifle and inhibit the flow and too little can dissipate it into the ether. Someone usually needs to be in charge of direction, even when it is minimal.

I, Sedonia, learned much about the use of structure and direction from attending the Long Dances led by Elizabeth Cogburn. She is not afraid of taking charge. She learned how to lead powerful ceremonials by going to the New Mexico pueblos and observing their dances. She did not go to learn what they did but how they did it: their timing, organization, and cooperation.

During her all-night dances when she sees the energy and enthusiasm ebb she uses the drum and the sound field to reawaken the group. In the three days prior to the dance she uses the cabala and the Tree of Life to form a matrix for the dance. She also teaches specific movements that encourage yin and yang energy and in this way she directs the balance of female and male energy in the group. The yin dance moves in a counterclockwise direction and is slow, horizontal, and flowing. The yang dance moves clockwise and is fast, vertical, and energetic. She insists that these movements continue at all times so that the dance does not become unbalanced by either the yin or yang energies.

In my own work taking people out on vision quests into the desert I find it necessary to create a safe and well-structured foundation so that the questers can feel secure enough to go to their solitary mountaintops and enter the unknown. Much of the foundation is created through well-defined circles where we do specific work in preparation for the alone time on the mountain. In some ways these people place their lives and welfare in my hands and it is necessary for me to be responsible for the decisions and circle crafting at base camp.

During these quests circling is used to clarify intentions and provides a context to speak of fears and how to deal with them. We sit in circle while the questers are instructed in the making of a sacred fire, which we all build together in a ceremonial way. In this way they learn how to build a fire that honors and respects the delicacy of the desert, as well as personal safety. We also sit in circle while I instruct them in other safety precautions necessary to survival in the desert. When their solo times are complete we sit in circle to hear each person's personal vision story and be witness to his or her achievement and discoveries. Each of these circles is structured, yet it allows a place for the individuality of each participant.

I have learned from circling during vision quests that the questers can feel free enough to enter the unknown and find their own source of internal power when they feel that the structure of the base camp supports that. Well-defined and purposeful circles form the foundation of that support. This same principle applies in all the ceremonial work I am responsible for.

Simplicity

In circle and ritual making it is good to follow the law of simplicity. Often people who are new at circle crafting will have a tendency to make their circles very complex, including everything imaginable in one circle. Good circles and ceremonies are actually very simple and elegant. It is good when there is no real need for spoken instructions, and the leader can lead by example. If things are too complex this is not possible. It is also good to leave plenty of space for the unexpected, leaving room for everyone in the group to feel they are part of the co-creation. When the leader knows how to hold and maintain the energy of the circle lots of room can be made for Spirit to enter. Again, this can not happen if the circle is too complicated. Songs should be simple enough for everyone to be able to join in after hearing them once or twice. It is better not to give people parts to read, but rather to encourage them to speak, pray, or invoke from the inner inspiration of the moment.

Clarifying your intentions will usually result in simplification of the circle. Overly cluttered and complex circles are usually the result of unclear intentions. It is a good idea to begin circles by stating your intentions and asking others in the circle to state theirs. This helps everyone to stay focused and on track.

QUESTIONS TO ASK WHEN YOU BEGIN A CIRCLE:
These are some questions that can help you to determine the structure of a circle.

1. What is the intention? Why is the circle being called? What is its
   purpose?
A good way to answer this is to clarify the vision that has inspired you to call a circle. Ask yourself why it is important to you to meet with others in a circle at this time. What is the larger purpose that you hope to serve?

2. Who is to receive the call?
Are there specific people you want to reach? Perhaps it is family members,

or neighbors, or a group of people in the healing professions, or mothers with small children. Perhaps it is just women or just men. It could be a group of people who are all facing a similar crisis, or who share a common life-style or vision.

One circle that we know about that takes place in San Francisco was convened for the purpose of brainstorming and is open to anyone who wants to participate. The people who come to the brainstorming circle all need a format to bounce their creative ideas off of other people in an atmosphere of support. One of the specific rules of this circle is that no idea or vision is considered too far-out or ridiculous.

3. Where will the circle meet?

When a circle meets in the same place for a period of time the place becomes energized by the circle. A powerful vortex of energy is created that supports all subsequent circles. The vortex can help the work of the circle go deeper and become more clear. It is as if the earth itself responds to the conscious attention. It is only necessary to enter one of the ancient circular kivas in the Southwest or walk among the megaliths at Stonehenge to realize the truth of this.

Determining the place where a circle will meet has a lot to do with defining its structure. If it meets at the home of the convener, more responsibility naturally falls on that person. If the circle meets outside, in nature, the boundaries are not so well defined. Sometimes circles meet in specific places to experience the unique quality of that place. Sometimes circles meet to highlight a concern as when a group of people made a circle around the Pentagon.

The meeting place should be prepared carefully; it should be clean and orderly. Lighting is very important. In the evening, candlelight lends an air of magic. Remember, you are creating an atmosphere that will be conducive to entering the sense of sacred time and space.

4. What is the date and time of the circle? How many hours will the circle meet?

A circle can be called to meet only one time to celebrate and acknowledge a special occasion or it can be ongoing. You may want to call a circle to celebrate a birthday, wedding, birth, or any life transition. My women's circle meets each month on the new and full moon. There is a circle that meets on Mount Shasta only once a year on the Aquarian full moon of August.

In selecting the time of day for a circle to meet, consider the practical needs of the group. However, if you have a choice you may want to take into consideration the different ambience of day and night. Some circle work is enhanced by the daylight, others by the darkness. The Native American Church begins its prayer circle at sundown and continues until the dawn.

5. Will the circle be ongoing?

When a circle meets regularly over a long period of time it allows for inner work that is not possible otherwise. Making a commitment to meet regularly bonds the participants. The act of commitment in itself can produce growth. Meeting regularly engenders a level of intimacy and trust. Such meeting is the first step in creating an extended family and clan.

6. Will the circle be an open or closed membership? How will the members be selected? What will the members have in common with one another?

This is really one of the most difficult questions to grapple with in circle making. Sometimes it is necessary to say no to someone who may want to join your circle, and though it is painful and uncomfortable to do so it can be for the benefit of the whole group. Some people can be too distressed to be a member of a circle unless the circle is specifically oriented toward healing.

We have both found that it is sometimes important to meet in gender-specific circles. Both women and men need to meet with their own gender to do certain kinds of work. This seems especially so for people who are coupled as it allows a release from prescribed patterns of behavior that are so often dictated by gender roles.

7. Will there be a leader or will it be leaderless? If there is a leader will the leadership rotate among the members? What will be the duties of the leader? If it is leaderless how will the group make decisions?

For many this is a philosophical question. Some people are opposed to having any hierarchy at all. However, to form a circle someone has to be responsible for initiating it, although the convener does not have to be the leader.

Whether there is to be a leader depends on the purpose of the circle. Someone who calls a circle for a special event may want to lead it, or invite someone else to do so, especially if a particular ritual that requires special guidance is involved. Circles that are for teaching or therapy usually have a leader.

When I, Sedonia, am teaching, even when it is in an academic institution, I do it in circles whenever that is at all possible. Even though it is done in a circle I am, however, still in charge. Years ago in San Francisco, when I regularly attended Alyssium, it was loosely led by four women therapists. They were in charge but everyone's participation was full.

The leader/convener has certain practical responsibilities, such as being sure that everybody has proper directions to the meeting place. It is often helpful to have a phone tree where each member is responsible for calling one other member to notify her or him of any change of plans. This may sound elementary, and it is, but such considerations are necessary for the functioning of a cohesive group.

The lodges we belong to are leaderless, which works in an ongoing and committed group with well-defined guidelines. For a leaderless group to work everyone has to be willing to take responsibility, to be free and spontaneous, and have a willingness to sit with nothing happening until someone feels directed by Spirit. Sometimes nothing happens and that has to be okay too.

RITUAL MAKING

Ritual is a component of ceremony. The ceremony is like a canvas and the ritual the color to be added. Ritual can be done unconsciously; there is no magic technique for waking up and being present, but when ritual is done consciously it adds a beautiful texture to a ceremony.

Some circles come together for the express purpose of enacting a rite of passage in a ceremonial way; birth, marriage, puberty, menopause, divorce, children leaving home, jobs begun or ended, significant birthdays, moving, communities forming or dissolving, and death are just some of the reasons for creating a special ritual. To co-create a rite-of-passage ritual in a circle of friends is to have loving witness and support for the changes that are being acknowledged. To witness is to share and in this way all in the circle are enriched. Circles are ideal containers for ritual because they provide the encouragement and safety to support transformative actions.

Every ceremony is divided into three discrete parts that need to be honored and reconciled for the circle to touch us deeply. These are the same psychological processes that compose our lives. The circle provides a clarifying setting for us to make these processes better known and understood. It is designed to enlarge and expand our sense of the sacredness of the ordinary.

1. Severance is the act of moving from the world of our habits into sacred ceremonial time and space.
2. The Threshold/Liminality phase is the heart of the circle, when we go beyond ourselves, leaving behind our limited identities. The alchemical

effect of being in this phase in a circle brings forth a part of ourselves that we had not known existed.

3. Reincorporation is a process of returning to the "everyday world" with new self-knowledge, and a way to integrate and use that knowledge in daily life.

Some of the Rituals that go into Creating a Meaningful Ceremony are:

Prayer	*Burning Objects*
Invocations	*Burying*
Use of Incense	*Untying or Tying*
Use of Smoke	*Washing*
Special Gestures	*Knocking Down Objects*
Offerings	*Ordeals*
Use of Power Objects	*Building & Lighting Fire*
Fasting	*Movement within and without Circle*
Feasting	*Mimetic Acts*
Making Taboos	*Wearing Masks*
Music	*Use of Special Power Name*
Singing/Chanting	*Wearing Symbolic Clothing*
Ritual Silence	*Crossing Thresholds*
Dance	*Purification*
Creation of Altar	*Handclasps/Embraces*
Vigils	*Exchanging Special Gifts*
Stress Induction	*Symbolic Death and Rebirth*
Lighting Candles	*Specially Induced Stress*
Breaking Objects	*Immersion in Water*

SPEAKING TO SPIRIT: *prayer, invocations, dance, singing, special gestures*

The purpose of ceremony is to connect with higher powers, allowing our bodies to be a conduit for the source of life. To stand alone, with outstretched arms, beneath an expansive sky or with a group of friends, and declare "I call on the powers of the Universe as my witness, hear my prayer!" is an expression of a powerful intention to speak with Spirit. On the island of Bali ceremonial dance and music are used to entice the Spirits to be present in their ceremonies.

We usually begin circles by calling in the directions, in this way casting or drawing the circle. Each of the directions has specific characteristics and qualities and these are called in to create a wholeness in the circle and a protective energy around it.

Women's hands become part of the altar. *Photo: Anthea Francine*

SACRIFICE: *fasting, ordeals, sleeplessness, stress, induction, vigils, making taboos, silence*

The word sacrifice means "to make sacred" and sometimes before one is ready or prepared to speak with Spirit it is necessary to give up some thing or behavior pattern that is binding. Temporarily giving up food, incessant talk, sleep, sex, or physical comfort sensitizes the body and opens one to what is really happening inside. Some believe that these practices make one transparent and because of this invite the entrance of Spirit.

WORSHIP: *altars, power objects, offerings*

At some ceremonies it is fitting to build an altar that expresses the intention and diversity of the participants. A serape or beautiful cloth can be laid on the ground and each circle member can carefully place an object that has special and symbolic meaning on it, using words to clarify its meaning for the group. For instance, people sometimes place crystals from their personal altars, or a piece of jewelry that they have worn for a long time, or a leaf from a tree that has had special significance to them. These objects get energetically "charged" from the ceremony and can then be used for healing purposes.

If a circle group decides to create an altar that will be permanent, it should be tended by one or more people. It should be smudged, blessed, and purified in some way on a regular basis. Perhaps it will need to be dusted, the candles changed, flowers placed there, or removed. Remember, it is a way of speaking to and honoring Spirit and the connection will be stronger if the altar is lovingly and carefully maintained.

EXORCISING: *breaking, untying, burying, burning, offerings, knocking down objects, cutting hair*

An important part of ceremony is a breaking away from the old, to make way for a new consciousness or behavior. One effective ritual is to make a list of your addictions and place them on a prayer arrow and burn them. This can be done alone or in a circle. Another exorcising ritual is building a pile of rocks, each representing a part of the past that you are ready to leave behind. This pile is then knocked down to represent commitment to moving on to the new.

PURIFICATION: *washing, immersion in water, smudging, prayer lodge*

Purification is a process of cleansing away the mundane and preparing to enter the sacred. When a ceremony is held by a body of water it provides the perfect environment to develop a unique baptism ritual. The Native American sweat lodge utilizes both fire and water to cleanse the body and mind of accumulated waste and to free the spirit.

COMMUNING: *music, singing, dancing, mimetic arts, ritual silence, incense smoke*

The purpose of ceremony is to commune with the depths of one's being and to align that source place with the natural world. Opening up the body and bringing forth sounds and movements that express the inner world is the most ancient way to commune with Spirit. Spirit responds to honesty; as long as the sound you make is true it will be heard and it will be pleasing. A dance might involve gestures that imitate, or mime, an animal that you wish to commune with and be empowered by. Another ritual that is used to commune with Spirit is to send one's prayers on the smoke from burning incense, or ceremonial use of tobacco or other herbs.

SYMBOLIC DEATH: *moving in and out of circle, crossing thresholds, symbolic death and rebirth, burying*

To cross a symbolic threshold or doorway into ceremonial time symbolizes the death of the old you. Moving back out through the threshold is a symbol of rebirth. One effective severance ritual is for the group to moan as the quester moves outside of the circle. Some native peoples practiced a ritual called "a night in the hole" in which they bury themselves up to their heads in the ground, as if dead, with a Medicine Person nearby.

CALLING THE LIGHT: *lighting candles, building fires*

When fire is used in a ceremonial way it is one of our most powerful tools. Sometimes vision questers have small fires in their circles during their solo times and will slowly feed it twigs and sticks that represent various parts of their bodies or psyches to be burned in the transforming fire. Sometimes people ceremonially burn an old garment that represents their old ways when they are ready to take on the new. In our winter solstice ceremonies each participant lights a candle to honor the returning light.

REBIRTH: *power name, masks, wearing symbolic clothing*

Sharing a name that you have chosen to represent your commitment to a spiritual path is to make a declaration of powerful intention that you are a new person. Many people use their power names only in ceremonial context and others make them their everyday names. Painting your face or wearing a mask can bring forth an archetypal part of yourself that you want the group to witness. It might represent an animal totem, a deity, or a member of your inner family.

COMMUNITY: *giving gifts, feasting, handclasps/embracing*

If communing with Spirit is the purpose of ceremony then community is the celebration of the communion. One of the greatest joys of circling is sharing what you have been able to create together as a tribe. To share food or gifts or touch is to honor the sacred space that has been co-created.

Some people share food in ritual by only feeding one another rather than feeding themselves. It is interesting to discover that a little food goes a very long way toward nourishing when it is given lovingly from another's hand.

These ritual tools can be used in many combinations. The important thing is that they be used in total mindfulness and awareness of their symbolic meanings for the individual and group. Their real purpose is to put us in touch with the archetypal world where all is sacred. In this way ritual helps us incorporate mythic dimensions into our daily lives and understand and accept big changes, or rites of passage, that occur at predictable intervals during our lives.

A potent use of ritual in circling was developed by Chellis Glendinning, a writer and therapist based in New Mexico, to deal with environmental despair. The ritual form consisted of three concentric circles. The outer circle was called the Circle of Information, a place for objectivity and a safe place for people who chose not to share their emotions. The next circle was the Circle of Anger and Fear, where it was safe to feel anger and express it by stamping feet, shaking, shouting. The inner circle was called the Circle of Sorrow. Here it was safe to cry, curl into a ball, and feel sadness.

The circle begins with everyone standing in the Circle of Information. After a few moments of chanting or singing together whoever is willing begins by sharing a fact or a feeling about the state of the world, "I hate that the oil companies are destroying the ocean." Then everyone in the circle says "So be it." Next everyone chants "Om" or any simple chant that opens the heart. During this process when one becomes aware of feeling fear, anger, or sadness they move into the appropriate circle and give vent to those feelings. Thus begins a dance from the inner to the outer circle as each person responds to the preceding person's concerns.

The individuals in the group usually discover they are not alone in their despair and anger and find they have been empowered through the process of opening their hearts to the concerns of others and feeling that their fears have been witnessed. It is best to end this circle on an optimistic note once the despair feelings have been reconciled. As part of the closing ceremony the circle members may agree to make an action contract, independently or jointly, to affect a change in the body politic.

Working with sound

Working with sound is a wonderful way to bring a circle together. You don't have to be an expert musician to utilize sound in unifying a group of people. All you need is the willingness to play and experience the pureness of spontaneous sound, which is fresh, rides the wind currents, and leaves no trace. Each circle will have a unique sound depending on the participants, the place, the time of year. At a summer solstice circle on the beach an eleven-year-old boy found a dried piece of seaweed and began blowing into it, making a perfect seaweed saxophone.

Everyone has a sound of his or her own. It is an exhilarating experience to bring your own original sound-expression into a circle. If you are unsure of the sound that is uniquely yours try vocalizing, using single vowels rather than words, while sitting in a bathtub or a pool of water or taking a shower. Let yourself experiment freely until you find your sound.

Another helpful exercise for finding your own sound can be done with a partner. While sitting opposite each other one person begins to play with her or his voice making a wide variety of spontaneous sounds. The other person simultaneously repeats the succession of sounds, which requires a sensitive listening. This exercise is both fun and freeing for the fifth chakra, that region of power and interface with the outer world that so many of us have blocked in order to conform.

In our circles we usually begin with drumming and rattling and let the sound field form the foundation of the circle. The drums bring in the energy of the earth and the rattles call in the spirit realm. While the drums are sounding we weave our voices into the steady beat. We often use our voices in individually free and spontaneous chanting. The feeling tone is primal. This is a time for people to allow whatever sounds are within them to be released. The content of the sounds is secondary, though words may be used, and sometimes beautiful call and response patterns develop.

Don't worry if you have never drummed before, just go out and get a drum. We use drums from India, Africa, America, China, India, Mexico, and the Middle East. The first thing to learn about drumming is to keep a steady beat, even a simple one like one-one-one-one. When you play with other people the key is to listen and to establish a sound-dialogue with one another.

An effective method we use for leading a circle of beginning drummers is for one of us to begin drumming alone, asking the person on our left to join us with his or her drum when he or she has really heard our beat. Then the person on his or her left is asked to do the same, listening attentively for a few minutes to the preceding drummer. And so on around the circle until everyone is drumming together. We usually stop the drumming in the same pattern it was started.

Elizabeth Cogburn uses a huge council drum to lay the ground and hold the pulse for all her ceremonies. During her annual sun dance the drum never misses a beat for the three days and nights the dance is happening. Days after the ceremony has ended you can hear the drum echo wherever you go.

Music can induce an altered state and is the main component of many healing rituals from around the world. One effect of repetitious drumming and singing is to produce a trancelike state. While such a state can be used harmfully, as in military entrancement, it can also be used for healing when it is focused with love and caring.

There is an art to reading the sound energy of the circle. There is a time to be still and a time to be active. Just as the silence between the

Women drummers at the Women's Summer Solstice Camp in northern California. *Photo: Patricia Waters*

notes defines the melody, so too, the silence between expression defines the emotional quality of a circle. It is important not to hurry, to let silence punctuate the spaces between what is articulated.

Silence is an essential part of the sound field created in the circle. Sometimes after drumming and singing has reached a crescendo it is good to stop and allow silence to fill the space. One of the most important lessons of circling is learning to contain silence and feel the fullness of its grace as well as its emptiness. Being able to contain is directly proportional to being able to express. If one is uncomfortable with silence there will be a triviality of expression. There is a potency of silence when shared in a circle that helps in maintaining spiritual practice while alone. Being able to sit in silence builds a personal reservoir of energy that deepens the power you bring to the circle.

Some circles come together for the purpose of singing. Singing together is a sure way for a group of people to bond. Some songs have been borrowed from traditional cultures and others are being created from the new circles. A fascinating phenomenon of circling is the way that new songs circulate and evolve as they pass from community to community.

Name Singing

In a new circle singing can be used to introduce members to one another. One member begins by singing his or her name to the group and the group responds by repeating it just as it was sung. Sometimes, if the group is playful, they will improvise with the name, repeating it many times, each person singing in an individual way. Name singing can also be used when a person needs healing energy. This person moves into the center of the circle, either sits or lies down with eyes closed, and the group sings his or her name over and over. There is something very transformative and deeply emotional about hearing one's name sung out loud by a group of friends.

WORKING WITH THE ENERGY FIELD

When a circle is formed with a clear intention, and the pulse of dancing, singing, or drumming is deep, an energy field is established that, though invisible to the untrained eye, is nevertheless present.

Traditional tribal people are able to create and maintain a very powerful ceremonial energy field for extended periods of time because they are living in a cohesive culture. Their houses are shaped the same, their garments are handmade in similar styles, they eat the same food, they learn to drum, dance, and sing from watching their parents and relatives, just as they had watched theirs. All of their ceremonial ways are inspired by the natural environment that they live in. Their ceremonial arts are part of a strong morphogenetic field that is strengthened from centuries of use.

We, on the other hand, come from a diverse, multicultural, and often fragmented background. Often we circle with people whose life-styles are very different from ours. What needs to be done to make a common ground and to hold a strong ceremonial energy is to make decisions that are good for the group while maintaining a sense of self. If everyone can hold his or her own internal power, while being sensitive to the group, the circle will be a conduit for a strong, flowing energy.

It is important to be aware of the way the group is facing in a circle. If everyone is facing inward the energy is contained, whereas if the intention of the circle is to send a message, for example at a world peace healing meditation, then it is important to face outward. In such a circle you would want to begin by facing inward and use the sound field or a group meditation to build a high charge and then face outward to send the healing vibrations out to the world.

Another law of circling is based on an awareness of solar and lunar principles. Solar energies move downward and spiral through the circle in a clockwise motion on their way to the earth. Lunar energies come up from the earth and spiral through the circle in a counterclockwise motion and upward to the heavens. If you want to build a concentration of energy it is best to dance, move, or pass the talking staff in a clockwise direction. If you wish to diffuse or release the energies, movement should be counterclockwise.

The way energy moves through the circle will vary with the seasons, the time of day, and the phase of the moon. In winter nature and people go inward and the energy of a circle is usually deep, quiet, and introspective. In the summer the energy is more outgoing and active and the energy in the circle will usually reflect this.

Daytime circles are often best when devoted to psychological processing, decision making, and consciousness work. Nighttime circles are good for working on dreams and the unconscious, exploring mystery and magic, working with the nonverbal and the mind-altering, entering the realm of Spirit.

Sometimes when the moon is dark we don't speak in our circles, except through singing or sounding. This is to honor the absence of moonlight and the deep silence that always seems to accompany that absence. It is also a way to acknowledge and honor the depth and the nonlinear mode of our personal experiences at that time of the monthly cycle. When the moon is full we interrelate in a verbal and more celebratory manner.

COMMITMENT

If an ongoing circle is to continue it requires commitment from the members. Perhaps the single most important thing about creating a circle is to be there . . . and be there . . . and be there . . . and be there. Even when nobody comes, if your intention is strong and you are willing to be there no matter what, the circle will finally come together.

When a circle forms with an intention to be ongoing it is a good idea, after a few meetings, to design a ceremony in which each person declares a commitment to the circle and makes a ritual gesture of that commitment. When members decide that it is time to end their circle commitment it is good if they can design another ritual to make their reasons for leaving clear to the group. If this doesn't happen it will leave an energy tear in the circle-basket that the remaining members will have to reweave.

When members of an ongoing circle become lax in their commitment and allow all manner of excuses to keep them away, it causes a rupture in the circle. It is a good idea to ask people to be clear about their commitment and if they must miss a meeting ask them to send some energy to the circle at the time it is meeting so that the circle can be strong and whole.

The technologies of circle making are ancient and rely upon instincts and knowledge we all have deep inside us. All these technologies are subservient to three principles of circle making: clarity of intention, honoring, and commitment. A successful circle depends upon clear intention, but such intention is directly connected to honoring. It is important, in circling, to honor all of life as a part of the circle and in this manner not to be cut off from the real purpose of circling.

THREE

TOOLS OF THE CIRCLE

In a circle of fire, in a circle of fire,
Come together, come to sing, come to this night.
from a song by BETSY ROSE

The technology of the sacred involves the ability to invoke, heal, bless, speak, write, dance, and drum. The visionary and the backward-dancing-around-the-fire-the-wrong-way coyote are both faces of the shamanic technician. The tools are part of a morphogenetic field of ceremonial practice because they have come out of thousands of years of one-hearted development and use. The tools deserve respect because they hold the *baraka*, the loving energy charge of other women and men who have walked the Rainbow Path through time.

CASTING THE CIRCLE

To make a circle is to locate ourselves in the center of the universe by acknowledging that the time is *now* and the place is *here*.

To make the circle a safe container, a basket wherein all kinds of life-affirming things can happen, we begin by calling in the powers of the directions. This is done to invite the archetypical qualities of the cardinal points, that they might bear witness, lend support, and impart wisdom to our endeavors. This acknowledges that we human beings need help, that we need to cross the limited boundaries of ego into the essential oneness of *self*. This aligns us and our intentions with the larger impulses of life.

One way of doing this is to have people sitting or standing in each of the four directions light a candle as they call out to the powers of their direction. The one in the east might invoke the Spirit of the rising sun, asking for new beginnings and far-reaching visions for the circle. The person in the south could call for the warmth of the noonday sun to open the hearts and renew the trust and innocence of the group. The west might call forth the setting sun to carry everyone present into the deeper recesses of looking within, and the north might invite the calm quiet of midnight where experience becomes wisdom. Another person might call in the below, the Earth Spirit, to hold and support the circle, to impart patience and nurturing, then someone can call the Sun Spirit to bring forth the nurturing of warmth and light.

In casting a circle we also often call in the spirit powers of all the animals, birds, plants, trees, waters, ancestors, and those yet unborn so that all of life is present and considered. In this way we humans begin to find our way back into the Sacred Hoop that we abandoned so long ago.

In the mandala of our psyche there are many currents, patterns, and images. It is the intention of the circle to bring forth currents of thought and feeling that engender vastness, the big mind, the whole picture.

In some circles people may feel a need to call in specific helpful attributes, such as the mother bear's spirit in fighting for her cubs, the cougar's spirit of courage and grace, the owl's way of seeing the light in the darkness, the tree spirits for standing tall and steady, the plants for the spirit of generous giving, the wind spirit for movement and change.

This circle song beautifully calls forth these qualities:

Animals spirits come to me now
Vanishing ones, come and live within me.
When I run let me run like a deer.
When I fight let me fight like a mother bear.
When I hide let me hide like a fox.
Learn to strike like a rattlesnake.

Some call in the spirits of all the ancestors, the grandmothers and grandfathers, both known and unknown, to bring comfort and wisdom to the circle.

There are those who cast a circle by sprinkling cornmeal, tobacco, or living water around the outer perimeters of the group to create a boundary and seal in the energy. Some say that the ancient grandmothers are attracted to the circle by cornmeal and the grandfathers by the tobacco. In some pagan circles a broom is swept around the edges of the circle to symbolically clear away all negative influences.

When it is time to close the circle it is important to thank all the

A women's circle around an altar. *Photo: Anthea Francine*

energies and spirits that were invited to be present and ask them to walk with us as we move into the larger circle of our lives.

MODES OF PRAYER

As one becomes more involved with circle work and earth-centered ways, the understanding of prayer is expanded to include singing, dancing, drumming, walking, eating. Anything done with respect, mindfulness, and Spirit consciousness is a form of prayer.

Imagine an elder whose path has been good and full experiencing life as a continuous prayer. Picture a person standing at the top of a hill, outstretched arms holding a medicine pipe, in total intention and at-

tunement with the Great Spirit. One can imagine this intimacy of speaking with Spirit on a one-to-one basis, like an old friend who is known very, very well. Now, picture a dozen or more people sitting on the earth in a tight, dark prayer lodge, perspiration on their hot bodies making the ground wet and muddy. There is something very childlike and innocent about being naked and huddling with friends in the womb of the lodge. Now imagine a group of circle dancers, intent and synchronized, placing each foot consciously on the earth-altar, or a peace walker crossing this globe on foot, making each footfall a prayer for peace.

Many shamanic tools are used to engender states of prayer. Smudging, drumming and singing, the talking staff and other ritual tools are all, when used properly, forms of prayer.

Smudging

Native peoples all over the earth use burning herbs for purifying space and one another. Smudging is a word sometimes used for this purifying smoke ceremony. Typically an abalone shell, a bowl, or a hollow rock is filled with leaves from a dried herb that are lit and the fragrant smoke is spread around the room with a special feather. One person can smudge each individual in the circle by wafting the smoke around each one using the special feather, or the shell can pass from person to person, each smudging the one to her or his left. Several plants can be used: dried desert sage for cleansing and purifying, dried cedar for balancing body, mind, and spirit, dried lavender for walking the beauty way, and braided sweet grass for conferring blessings.

Smudging has many effects on the individual and collective psyche. It serves as a demarcation of time, notifying everyone present that Sacred Time is beginning. It is a signal for the mind to be still and in present time. One of the profound attributes of smudging that makes it an important tool for circlers is that it provides everyone in the group with a shared sensual experience. As the sweet-smelling smoke encircles the area it is easy to feel the presence of Spirit entering and filling all those present.

Some believe smudging with feathers of different birds produces differing results. Hawk feathers are used to encourage vision and inspiration. Owl feathers are believed to bring deep insights about oneself and often seem disruptive to people who are afraid of examining their shadow side. Many tribes have a taboo against their use, but like menstrual taboos, these are being reinterpreted. Eagle feathers are usually reserved only for those who are in leadership roles, as they confer a certain responsibility on the user. Any large feather, such as wild turkey, that is beautiful and special can be used.

Feathers can be found wherever the birds make their habitats or from road kills. If you find a bird that has been killed by a car and you decide to take the feathers it is important to do so in a way that is respectful. When you lift the bird from the ground it is important to leave an offering in its place. The feathers should be plucked or the wings cut off with a sharp knife. Salt should be placed on the parts of the bird that you plan to keep. The remaining parts should be buried along with offerings of cornmeal or tobacco as you make prayers of gratitude to the bird's spirit for giving away to you.

Make a promise to use the feathers in a good way and thank Spirit for this blessing and gift. Many bird feathers are illegal in North America and you can be fined for possession of them unless you are a Native American and have a permit to have these feathers. It goes without saying that it would be extremely unethical to kill a winged one to obtain its feathers.

THE DRUM

I, Joshua, think of the drum as the trumpet of the earth, a trunk of a tree voluntarily come back alive to be renewed on the pulsating cord of culture. It is the voice of the earth coming through to speak in the universal language of the heart. Drumming is tribal music; that drums have reappeared is part of the natural expression of people reclaiming their original essence.

One of the first things to focus on in drumming is finding the base. The base is the lowest, earthiest tone and is found in the middle of the drum. It is

Women playing a large council drum at the Women's Summer Solstice Camp. *Photo: Patricia Waters*

the sound of the center of the circle. It can only be found when people are grounded. To find the base it is helpful to have a dancer present. Ask the dancer to stamp her or his left foot on the ground in a scratch and stamp motion, as if her or his foot were a paw. Another way to determine and lay down the base is by echoing the pattern of sound made by the movements of a body engaged in natural activity: swinging a hoe, working on a loom.

The base is the pulse of the beat, the earth coming through the dancer. Finding the base is part of an elaborate communication, an unbreakable alliance, between drummers and dancers. One of the innate powers of the drum is to call in Spirit by drawing awareness into the earth, into the body. This is one of the best ways to get reconnected with the roots.

The drum has the potential, if its base is understood, if the base is found correctly, to resonate the body-temple into a state of deep feeling and fertility, where the energy of the organism opens up in pure, synergistic channels. The base tone has the power to knit the wounds in the psyche by calling upon The Presence of The Present. This requires a very pronounced state of muscular vitality, spiritual remembering, and mindfulness. The entire nervous system is involved in the sensing of the structure and the intuiting of the base. The pulsing pattern of The Presence is always made for the first time and is connected to the original pulse.

It is good to drum in many situations and feel the common pulse. The purpose of the drum is to speak so that a common tone can be found among everyone. It is important to study other traditions but it is just as important to hear your own, untamed wild beat. The pulse and base of shamanic drumming will vary with the temperature, the season, the time of the moon, the altitude, longitude, and attitude of the gathering.

The Legacy of the Drum

Each land has a legacy of sound, a collected unconscious of aural vibrations. The land I learned to play on has a story in its clay, a message in its hide, a remembering in its resonance. This is how it went. First there was the shaman's drum, then the shaman's drum was silenced. Then there was the slaves' drum, which was also confiscated because when the Africans drummed they remembered their native tongues and a fire would break out in the main-house kitchen.

The pulse of these two traditions was taken up and became a beat, a sound progression. Rock and roll came from African religious music and had a fury and a vision that would vitalize the whole world.

When you listen close enough you can hear the shaman's base, an exalting of the Oneness of Spirit, right up from the ground. The drum beckons an authentic liberation and turns theology into something real.

When I listen to the essence of America's sound I hear the songs of many people filtering through the mist. This is the shamanic ensemble, it settles and out of it comes something else. The best name for it is World Beat. These are the basic drums of the ensemble.

Dumbek: This is a Middle Eastern drum that can be adapted to fit any bio-region. Wherever anybody has a pottery studio, fine dumbeks can be produced. Putting the head on is very difficult but there are many people who know how. Go to one and find out. That act is a networking. The whole act of making drums is part of drumming. In every area there can be drums produced that are best suited to that place.

Conga: The renaissance of the drum is best witnessed through the conga. In many cities and towns there are places where people gather to play. Most music stores have congas for sale and most areas, if you ask around, have indigenous makers of these drums. In many renewal communities African dance classes have become a healing force for the people and there are always groups of fine drummers who play for the classes.

Two-headed Prakashe and Mrdungum: These drums are from India. They can be played standing up, strapped over the shoulders. They are used in the dancing, chanting, ecstatic tradition of worship.

Tabla: This Indian drum is a derivative of the two-headed drum adapted to a more classical setting. It is the two-headed drum cut in half and placed on the ground.

One-headed Native: There are many varieties of this basic drum. It can be made with as many sides as desired or round. There is one made with a synthetic head, which is inexpensive and is very practical for ceremonial use when it is foggy or damp. The synthetic head does not absorb moisture the way a natural-headed drum does. The drum head has to be tight to get good sound.

Taos Round Drum: This makes one of the finest base tones in the whole world. Every group should have one. It can be played by more than one person. I like to play it with a stick in each hand, kneeling on the ground. This is the sound of healing.

SITTING IN COUNCIL AND USING THE TALKING STAFF

One of the important uses of the circle is to find consensus or, as the Quakers say, the sense of the meeting. To sit in council in a circle allows an opening of heart and mind to new possibilities of understanding. It provides the opportunity to be really heard. All the participants agree to speak from their hearts and listen with their hearts in order to come to a

The talking stick is passed in a council circle at a Sun Dance. *Photo: Elizabeth Cogburn*

deeper understanding of themselves, one another, and whatever is being discussed. Such communication is very needed.

Brooke Medicine Eagle had this to say about the circle council:

A part of finding consensus in a circle is that rather than everyone looking at the speaker, all look into the center. In the olden days, the tribe often had a transforming fire in the center of the circle, which connected everyone to a deep, centered place. The fire represents the Great Spirit, which lies at the heart of everything.

This deep level metaphor brings recognition that there is a place where consensus and harmony rest, and that the discussion will draw the circle closer and closer, until it is one with all present as well as with All-That-Is. It is a way of creating a deep ecology. The discussion goes around and around the circle, until all are finally in agreement.

The most powerful and useful person in the circle, the one who comes to be respected as an effective leader, is not one who can forcefully carry an oppositional view, but one who can bring together into a unified, agreeable whole what everyone before her/him has expressed. This kind of process, possible in a circle, creates an atmosphere of cooperation, unity, and oneness, all attributes which we two-leggeds are being asked to make real in a personal, social, and spiritual sense now on Mother Earth. Thus, circle council is a very powerful, useful, timely, and simple tool.

One helpful way to get a new circle going is to introduce a question to which all the participants can respond. The question can be introduced into the circle in several ways. One good way of beginning is to discuss the intentions of the members. Answering this question may fill the entire meeting but it will help the group clarify its purpose. At other times a person can initiate a question about some issue that is vitally important to her, about which she wishes to have the group's input. In this manner the members of the group can serve as outer representatives of one another's inner council. Or perhaps a question concerning the welfare or direction of the group needs to be examined from many perspectives. Sometimes the questions are large and abstract, sometimes small and personal. Sometimes there is no agenda and the council time is used for people to share what is most important to them at the moment.

The talking staff is a tool that is used in council to facilitate communication. It is the wand of authority. Whoever holds the staff has the total focus and attention of the group. The staff can be a specially carved and decorated stick, a crystal, a feather, a flower, or anything that the group decides upon. Some use a vertically held stick to represent the unity of earth and sky. Some people use a crystal because it has the ability to amplify whatever anyone is feeling. A feather is used to carry the thoughts expressed to Spirit. A Medicine Pipe is used by some tribes to remind the participants of the sacredness and importance of the council. A flower is used to acknowledge the beauty and delicacy of the open heart. A simple unadorned stick or a rock that is found spontaneously for such an occasion can also be used and serves as a reminder to the circle of the simplicity of speaking and sharing from the heart.

The staff can move around the circle in two different ways. It can be passed from one speaker to the next in a clockwise direction or, after each speaker has finished, it can be placed in the center of the circle and picked up when the next person is ready to speak. The staff can be passed around once or many times. An important rule of the staff is that no one is to interrupt the person holding it. This is not the place for guessing what someone is going to say before he or she says it, for judging, fixing, or saving. The commitment is to sit and listen from a neutral and loving attitude, allowing the speaker the freedom to be really heard.

The importance of the talking staff is that it enables everyone to have a chance to speak, instead of allowing those with agile tongues to dominate the circle. We have seen shy and withdrawn people gain a new sense of self-assurance after speaking with the talking staff. It is a sad fact of contemporary life that many people, even as children, never had anybody listen to them or were rushed every time they had something to say. Don't rush the talking staff council. To speak from the depths of the heart can be difficult for those not accustomed to it and it can't happen if time is being measured.

The talking staff is an important tool for creating Sacred Time. It stops the world and ushers in a new time frame. In order for the talking staff to work, both the speaker and the listeners need to be in present time. This requires listening from the heart, which means listening from a neutral, nonintervening, compassionate space. Compassion is not sympathy, which is an overidentification with another's process; rather, it is a state of nonjudgmental witnessing.

The feeling of compassion that gets generated as the talking staff circulates is a very important part of circling. We live in a world that cultivates separateness between people. Such separateness can be palpably experienced as an illusion, when the magic of the circle is active. As the talking staff is passed from hand to hand, it becomes evident how much we are all concerned with the same issues and connected to the same Great Spirit. This state of compassion is the building block of community. It is also the foundation upon which a proper relationship to oneself is developed. Spiritual maturity, which is the ability to actualize love, to be loved, is based on compassion. Without compassion, even actions that seem to be for the benefit of others or oneself are intrinsically meaningless.

The talking staff reminds us that to speak is a privilege. Words are Sacred. They are Magical. They can be builders or destroyers, bringers of peace or hurtfulness. For many people the tongue is the most intransigent organ of the body, seemingly with a will of its own. To select one's words with care and thoughtfulness is to speak in a sacred manner. The talking staff helps us awaken from the stupor of too many words and of good words that have been used in evil ways. It is one of the most important tools of the circler.

In the beginning, a tendency of most people is to be so engrossed in rehearsing what they are going to say when the staff reaches them, that they are virtually unable to hear what is being said by others. Rehearsed speeches have their place but not in circles. They usually sound stilted and uninspired. The point is to allow Spirit to speak through you when the staff reaches your hands. This usually takes time and experience, so be easy on yourself. If you find your mind rehearsing, just take some deep breaths and focus on the speaker. The speaker, like you, deserves to be heard. In this way you honor yourself, the speaker, the circle, and Spirit. It is important to understand that when a member of the group speaks in a sacred and heartfelt way, your careful listening may reveal some previously ignored part of your own heart.

When Elizabeth Cogburn uses a staff in council she has a specific form. After the question has been decided upon, the first person holding the staff turns and faces the person on the left, looks into that person's eyes and says something like

> Do you love yourself enough to speak and listen with your heart to your co-hearts in this circle? If so can you tell us . . .

The person being addressed takes the staff and answers the question, and then passes it to the person to the left, repeating the question.

Another example of the use of the talking staff is in the Native American Church. Their prayer meetings are held in a circle, where both a staff and a rattle are passed clockwise. The staff is held in the left hand and the rattle in the right. The person holding the staff sings his or her song and accompanies him- or herself with the rattle, while the next person plays the drum.

THE RATTLE

Rattles call in Spirit. The contents of the rattle—beans, seeds, tiny crystals, or pebbles—represent the seeds of creation. To shake the rattle is to bring the seeds to life. When used alone it can induce a trancelike state. Vision questers often use rattles to stay awake all night on the mountain. You can rattle for hours if you keep your wrist loose. Holding and shaking the rattle in a vertical, up-and-down direction inspires and calls in yang, masculine energy; shaking in a horizontal, sideways motion brings a yin, feminine way. There is another way of shaking the rattle by making a fast, tight circle that produces a white, all-encompassing sound. When the rattle is used this way and held close to your ear it transports you out of the worldly and into a realm of spirit.

CIRCLE DANCING

Dancing is a primary way of singing to the earth. It makes a song that resonates through the body down into the earth, just as the earth sends its generous and healing resonances up through our feet. Dancing helps keep the earth in alignment and balance in the same way it keeps us. In circle dancing the purpose is to get into communion. There is a very

Women dance around the maypole at the Women's Summer Solstice
Camp. *Photo: Patricia Waters*

simple dance that involves all dancers moving their left foot to the left on
the first beat and bringing their right foot beside the left on the second
beat. This is done to the tempo of the drum, usually with everyone in the
circle facing the center. Such a dance can go on for hours and for days,
depending on the needs and intentions of the group. Sometimes the people
doing this dance hold brightly colored scarves that they sweep through
the air as they sway.

There was a time in the 1800s in North America when a revival
dance spread from a small village in Nevada all over the country. The
people gathered and danced to restore the ancient ways that were being
decimated by the conquering forces. It was called the Ghost Dance.
Thousands of people participated in it and though it did not restore
the tribal way of life or protect them from genocide, it provided a necessary spiritual experience and said to the earth, "we are people who
love you."

Community dances and celebrations are essential to the survival of a
people who are re-inhabiting the earth. Dancing can be woven into any

Spiral dance at a large Spring Equinox festival for healing the Earth. *Photo: Vicki Noble*

ceremonial circle when the physical space permits. The most important thing is for there to be permission and acceptance of dance as an expression of prayer, gratitude, and ecstasy.

Shields

Your circle might want to make a shield together and use it in a ceremony of commitment. Doing a project or making something together is an excellent way for a group to bond. You might want to make it soon after you have come together or wait until you have a firmer sense of who you are as a group.

It is important to make it with great care, understanding that it will be a sacred representation of your group. It tells the story of your group in symbols. You might want to begin with a small ceremony and chant or sing spirit songs as you make it.

The frame is usually made from the long, thin branches of the weeping willow tree (these are usually found near water). Alder or aspen or any tree with long, straight, pliable branches can be used. After you have respectfully asked the tree to take one of its branches, cut the branch as long as you want and immediately take a sharp knife and pull the bark off in long strips. You might want to tell the tree your intentions and leave a small offering in return for its generosity. Then immediately bend the branch into a circular or oval shape in the size that you want. You may have to do a lot of gentle coaxing if there isn't much sap in it. When it is the way you want it use the bark you have stripped off to tie the ends together. Allow this to dry for a few days.

You can make the face of the shield with soft leather, or canvas if you object to using animal hide. If you use a hide be sure to smudge it well and prayerfully thank the animal who gave away. The hide can be smaller in circumference than the frame, so that it is about one inch from it all the way around. Punch holes near the edge about two or three inches apart and use a long leather strip to lash it to the frame.

If you use canvas cut a circular piece that extends about two inches beyond the frame. Take a half-inch hem around the edge and place buttonholes every few inches near the edge. Use a long, strong thread, perhaps embroidery, to loop through the holes and pull tightly so that it is secure on the frame.

Designs can be painted on the face with leather or fabric paints, or you can paint it with natural substances, such as berries, tree barks, or various herbs. You can hang things from it, such as feathers, shells, small bundles, or anything that has meaning to you.

PRAYER ARROWS

A prayer arrow is a straight stick wrapped with yarn or ribbons in the colors of each direction: yellow for the east, red for the south, black for the west, and white for the north. As this is done prayers are spoken to the guardians of each of the directions. Feathers are placed on the prongs to carry the prayers to the Great Mystery.

One way to do this is to designate a prayer arrow as an addiction arrow. This involves listing all the things you are addicted to—substances, emotions, behaviors, objects, and people. In other words, the places and ways we leak our power. The list is tied to the arrow and, in an appropriate ceremony, the prayer arrow is carefully burned or buried, perhaps with the witness of the circle.

Another prayer arrow may be used for prayers of manifestation. This list includes acts of power, which are things we want to manifest in the next year or other time period. This prayer arrow is brought into one's habitat and placed on an altar or placed in one's garden.

Prayer takes many forms but the process is essentially the same, opening to gratitude and making a connection between the center of oneself and the universe. Prayer aligns the innermost self with the external world so that one has the ability and capacity to give thanks and praise. The effect of prayer is determined by the ability to go into the center of self. Unless this core of experience is touched the prayer remains superficial.

When people take supplicating postures, bowing, kissing the feet, kneeling, it is to remind the body of that crucial message, but such posturing only goes so deep. The real work of prayer takes place on a level that is invisible to the naked eye.

Healing ceremonies

One form of circle that utilizes many ritual tools is when people gather together for specific healing purposes. This use of the circle is perhaps the most widely known and used due to its effectiveness in initiating the healing response. There are many ways to format a healing circle and your group must find those which are best suited for your time and place. However there is nothing like holding the meeting outdoors, beneath the clear expanse of sky, near forest and meadow and running streams. Nature will endow your circle with its innate powers if you open up and let it in. Of course it is not always possible to be in nature, but since the circle is nature and contains the force and method of nature, the healing circle can be held indoors and still be a most effective tool.

One effective ritual for a healing ceremony is to have the person in need of healing stand or sit in the center of the circle and have all the participants sing the name of the one in the center. There is something amazingly potent about having a circle of friends sing your name. While this is going on, the one in the center may ask that focus be directed at a certain part of his or her body and for everyone to visualize it in perfect health and balance.

Another ancient rite for healing is a laying-on of hands. Again the person in need of healing goes to the center and each member of the circle places their hands gently on his or her body. It is good for the group to have been smudged or in some way ritually purified before doing this. Sometimes a few people in the group know the person better and they might choose to be nearest his or her head, or positioned at his or her feet. Once in a conducive position the group may chant a healing song, or *Om,* or sing the person's name, while visualizing her or him in balance and harmony.

Sometimes healing circles are held to heal a piece of the earth that has been ravaged by greedy exploitation. The earth responds to such healing just as the individual does. When a group of people gather in a woods that has been clear-cut, or a beach that has had oil drench its shore, or an orchard cut down to make way for parking places, it has an impact, though subtle. Just the acknowledgment seems to matter. Many times we have been at such ceremonies and a sign comes from Spirit that the nature deities have heard the collective remorse. A bird may circle the spot and speak its solidarity.

Healing council

For a community to be viable the energies between people need to be kept clean and clear. When conflict arises, as it will, the entire community is affected by it. It becomes the responsibility of the community to facilitate and encourage a healing between the aggrieved parties. If this does not happen the conflict festers and spreads a disease among the entire community. People begin to avoid one another, take sides, be drawn into codependent caretaking, gossip, and backstabbing. This has unraveled the fabric of many communities. The ability to resolve conflict is one that we have to discover anew; it is not part of our training. It can only be learned in the context of a community. If we can't heal within our own community how can we heal the world? If we can't stop the psychic violence among ourselves how can we put an end to war?

It does take courage to bring a conflict into a healing council. You have to be able to give up being "right" and instead be able to move from your position into a new way in which neither is really right or wrong, but instead recognized as a mirror and vehicle for one another's learning and moving into wholeness.

Purpose: The purpose of the healing circle is to create a safe environment for aggrieved persons to meet and be heard by those with whom they have an issue. The "issue" is evidence of a dysfunction between the individuals and therefore within the larger community.

Participants: Witnesses should be selected from the community by each principal to aid in the healing process of the council. The function of the witnesses is to support the healing process, rather than supporting either of the principals in being right or wrong. The witnesses need to keep the process on track by being faithful to the form chosen and to make certain that the aggrieved ones have really heard one another. Witnesses should stay in touch with their own feelings and leave themselves open to their own healing in this process.

Rules: There should be a commitment to confidentiality. Nothing witnessed should be spoken of outside the healing circle. The entire process needs to be framed in ceremony that acknowledges the sacredness of healing. The participants need to agree to see the process through to its conclusion. Optimally the group agrees to meet in an open-ended format, staying up all night if necessary to achieve a closure in the healing. An alternative is to have people commit to meeting more than once until the issue is cleared. All the participants must know that the time agreed on will be honored, otherwise the delicate process of interpersonal healing will be sabotaged.

It is agreed upon that the process is grounded in consensus and mediation. The principals need to stick to "I" statements rather than "you" statements. In other words, the principals can't say "you did such-and-such, you are a terrible person, you always do thus-and-so" but instead must stick to saying how they feel when certain things were said or done by the other one. The group could decide to delegate an allotted time-out from that rule so that feelings can be vented.

Everyone present should be aware that this is a process of healing for the entire group. The guidelines for witnessing should be kept, with no one taking sides, projecting onto, interpreting for, or caretaking. This will work best when all those present sit in their own circles of power, owning all their feelings and being present with their fears.

Plans should be made to provide for scheduled breaks during the process.

Process: Each principal and witness should receive a written statement of the desired intentions of the healing circle and a time should be set that is adequate and a place selected that will allow for uninterrupted privacy. There can be any number of witnesses but two or three selected by each principal is probably best. You might want to arrange for the entire community to be present on some occasions.

Sometime prior to the circle the witnesses should hold a meeting to make clear their intentions as witnesses, to discuss and agree to the rules, and to select a moderator. This is a time when they can acknowledge their responsibility, to whatever degree, as members of the community, to the impasse being dealt with in the healing circle. This is an issue of the community that stands in the way of whatever healing energy might come forth from the community.

The healing circle should begin with ceremony. There can be smudging of the space and all present, the powers of the directions called to witness and assist in the healing, and perhaps some drumming and singing. Someone should be delegated to smudge unobtrusively from time to time to keep the air clear and everyone on track and centered. A talking staff is then passed and group members state clearly their intention for being present.

At this point each principal in turn is given the staff and allowed an allotted amount of time to say what she or he is angry or hurt about, how she or he feels about the situation and the other principal(s) right at the moment. Then principals can be given an opportunity to put into historical perspective what happened to cause the disagreement. This is an opportunity to express hurt and anger and to have it clearly witnessed in the safety of sacred space. The group could then experiment with "you" statements here if that seems appropriate, as well as "I" statements, if anger needs to be released.

After this is completed each principal gets an opportunity to respond to the other's statement. The witnesses should make certain that each principal has heard what the other said. The witnesses can ask questions when it seems appropriate and helpful, with the moderator keeping an overall perspective. The witnesses' job at this point is to help facilitate clarity.

If this part breaks down the talking staff should pass among the witnesses, at which point they claim any threads they have to the story being discussed. This can be a valuable time for the witnesses to admit how their own personal dysfunctions relate to this situation, or perhaps another similar one in the past. Only experiences that seem totally relevant should be spoken of. This can help the principals get a broader and clearer perspective and feel supported enough to move from their positions. It acknowledges that we all make mistakes and have conflicts. It helps principals see their own misconceptions when they hear their trusted witnesses admit to theirs.

When this seems complete principals should be allowed to make a statement about what they want from the other principal(s). They should be encouraged to stay with this until they get down to what they really want, even if it is an impossible demand. It is healing to be able to express it and feel it heard. Each principal should respond with statements about what he or she can or can't do or give up, in response to what the other has stated he or she wants.

This is the time for the principals to state where they are with the process, how they are feeling about the disagreement and the other principals. The witnesses can also speak at this time about their process and say if they feel the air has been cleared sufficiently.

It is very important that the principals totally avoid statements about loving each other or displays of affection until this point in the process has been reached. It can be assumed that they care about one another and the community, otherwise they probably wouldn't have agreed to come into this healing circle. Loving statements spoken earlier in the process can be used to avoid dealing with the uncomfortable issues at hand and can be used to deflate the other's anger when that is the very thing that needs to be expressed and cleared before things can move forward. It is important in the council that everyone speak their fullest truth, and then it will be the time for speaking affection and conciliation, once the other is out of the way.

The closing ceremony should consist of brief statements from all those present if that seems necessary, the directions should be thanked, and perhaps a prayer offered. The group might want to share food together at this point to acknowledge the spirit of community and to congratulate themselves on a job well done.

If this cannot all be accomplished in one session a modified format can be used, being sure to begin and end each session with ceremony to honor the sacredness of the process.

PRAYER LODGE

The prayer lodge is a primary shamanic tool for prayer. A version of it was used by the natives in North America as a way of purifying and getting ready for ceremony and vision quests and other momentous events. It has been used in various forms all over the world.

The lodge is a large, round, inverted basket woven from long willow branches that are laced together with willow bark. It is made in such a way that it symbolizes the turtle, with the lodge itself being the body and with an altar mound made of dirt, representing the head. The mound/altar is placed about a foot outside and to the left of the lodge doorway with a column of earth connecting it to the body. There is a path from the lodge door to a fire pit a few yards away.

Inside the lodge there is a deep pit in the center, large enough to hold many rocks. The best rocks to use are volcanic because they are very porous, hold heat, and do not crack. River rocks should never be used because they splinter when they are heated. Rocks can be the size of a large grapefruit or larger.

There are usually four "rounds" in the ceremony. The lodge is covered with many tarps and blankets so that no light can get through and the arched doorway is covered in a manner that allows entry. Rocks that have been heated in a blazing fire in the fire pit are brought in at the beginning of each round and carefully placed in the pit inside the lodge.

The person who is leading the lodge ceremony decides how many rocks are needed and often makes that choice based on how cold the weather is and how hot he or she wants the lodge to be, and whatever sacred numbers he or she wants to evoke.

Then the fire keeper closes the door flap, the leader dedicates the lodge, and the staff is passed for the prayers to begin. When the lodge leader notifies the fire person and the flap is opened the first round is complete. After a pause for everyone to have water, which is passed in a clockwise direction after it is first offered to the spirits with prayers, more rocks are brought in, the flap closed, and the staff passed. This entire procedure is done four times, with each round dedicated to the powers of one of the directions.

When the people enter the lodge the movement is clockwise. Great care should be taken at all times not to step over the turtle's neck. Upon entering and leaving it is customary to touch the earth with the forehead and say "To all my relations" as a way of honoring and thanking all the rocks, tree branches, water, firewood, sage, and anything else that has given away in order for this ceremonial circle to occur. It is acknowledging that all these are our brothers and sisters, that their lives have great value and much was given.

The leader is responsible for holding the energy, calling in the spirits of each direction, deciding the focus of the prayers and songs, controlling the heat in the lodge, keeping the circle "on track," and deciding on the rules. When the rocks are first brought into the lodge the leader sprinkles them with a pinch of sage or other fragrant herbs, such as cedar, lavender, or sweetgrass, thanks the rocks, and asks for their assistance. Then the leader calls in the power of the direction that is being evoked and begins the round of prayers. As each person prays the leader sprinkles water on the hot rocks to create steam.

Usually people are not allowed to leave the lodge during a round and if someone has decided to leave between rounds he or she is not allowed to return. In such a circumstance the person is asked to stay outside the lodge with the fire keeper and hold silence around the lodge area.

In many communities where there is cultural renewal no taboo exists against women and men entering the sweat lodge together, or against menstruating women entering the lodge. Some people have rules about wearing clothes in the lodge and others don't care. Some sweat lodge leaders have different rules about these issues and the leader's rules and wishes should, of course, be respected when you are in his or her lodge or he or she has been invited to lead one in your community's lodge.

Sometimes women prefer to sweat solely with other women when they are bleeding. Some men prefer not to sweat with menstruating women, feeling that their power is too intense. Some prayer lodge leaders ask bleeding women to put their blood on the lodge entrance believing that the blood deserves to be honored and confers a special blessing.

The fire keeper's job is to build the fire in a sacred manner, about two hours before the sweat is to begin, with the rocks inside the fire so that they become red hot. When everyone is inside the lodge the leader gives the call and the fire keeper uses a pitch fork to bring the requested number of rocks into the lodge, placing them with great care into the pit so that no one is burned in the process. The fire keeper opens and closes the door flap when asked to by the leader and brings fresh drinking water into the lodge after each round. Between rounds the fire keeper tends the fire and maintains a spirit of silence and safety in the general area.

This ceremony, more than any other, seems to return people to their origins, to the mother's womb. In the dark, hot confines of the lodge, all the naked bodies huddled low and close, the hard dirt becoming mud when mixed with sweat, there is a depth that is both humbling and exhilarating. In the darkness people become almost anonymous, often their voices are hard to identify. All this seems to leave nowhere to go except deep, deep inside.

FOUR

FINDING YOUR PLACE
IN THE CIRCLE

We are crying for a vision that
all living things can share.
KATE WOLF

THE MEANING OF THE GREAT WHEEL OF LIFE

Teachings come in many forms. When people invest in a form that form
is enriched and attains an energy of its own; it becomes alive. The Great
Wheel of Life is one such vital form. It is an ancient circular symbol that
has been used by the native peoples for thousands of years. It is a kind of
mandala that represents the total universe and teaches us of ourselves and
our right relationship to all other living things. It shows us the path we
must all walk to be fully human. It shows us the way back to our home,
to our center.

The teaching is that we all enter life from one direction on the wheel.
Some enter from the south, some the east, others the north or the west.
We are born with a basic understanding of that part of the wheel. Our
life's task is to learn about the other three directions. This corresponds
to Carl Jung's theory of personality typing, which divides the mandala of
the personality into four distinct modes: thinking, feeling, sensate, and
intuitive. In his theory, as in the Great Wheel teachings, we are told that
we enter from one direction, our learning about two of the other directions
comes with relative ease, and learning to master the fourth can require a
lifetime of work. But learn it we must, as there is no other way to become
a whole and fully integrated human being.

We go around the wheel many times in each lifetime, learning and
refining what we already know each time, until we are finally so adept

that our movement becomes a dance. It is this dance that takes us to our rightful place in the center.

One simple way to learn of the wheel is to look at the four directions and their meanings:

The East is the place of sunrise and spring mornings. It is the place of beginnings and of vision. The ground has thawed, the seed is planted and begins to sprout. Here is the mountain where we go to seek vision and illumination and clarity. Here we fly on the wings of the eagle. In Jungian terms the function here is intuition. From the heights of the East we can see far into the future. It is here that the men sit in council. This is the place of Spirit, informed and energized by the fire of the sun. Here we learn that all we can imagine can be made real. It is the place of Spider Woman, continually creating and recreating the universe, teaching us that the weaver and the web are one.

The South is the place of innocence and trust. It is here we learn of emotion and passion. In Jungian terms this is the place of the feeling function. Here we learn to touch with our hearts, and to be touched. Here is the joy that we feel at noontime on a beautiful summer day. The animal of the South is the tiny mouse, always paying close attention to the smallest details of life. It is in the South that the musicians and the entertainers, the magicians and the ceremonialists teach us of beauty and magic. White Buffalo Woman, the bringer of the Sacred Pipe, comes from the South to teach the sacredness of all things. We can only understand Her message when we are totally in the moment and are willing to see once again through the eyes of a child. Only then can we see the world alive and shimmering, continually new and splendid. Only then can we feel our deep connection to all of creation.

The West is the place of inner work, of the women. Here the sun sets, the nighttime comes. This is the time to look deeply within, into the darkness to find the inner light. Here we touch the deepest part of our souls. Here the great mother bear goes into hibernation for the long winter. Here the snake sheds the skin it has outgrown. Here is the sensate function of the Jungians. The West is the place of Grandmother Earth and all she has to teach of cycles and change, of wisdom and patience, of decay and death and rebirth. It is the place of night and of the dream. It is the place of Changing Woman, with her constantly moving and flowing cycles, her continual rhythm of ebb and flow. It is here we learn of our responsibility to all living things and to the Earth, which has given us the gift of life.

The North is the place of winter time. The ground is frozen and in order to survive we must learn to cooperate with one another; we must learn of the Give-away. Here we understand that all the wisdom and knowledge and experience we have gained is not for ourselves alone but must be shared if we are to survive. The Jungian function is thinking. Here we learn to use the intellect in creative ways in which all things are honored. The animal of the North is the great buffalo, who gave all of itself so that the people might live, and the wolf who lived its whole life in the protection of the young and of its tribe. This is the lesson of the Grandmothers and Grandfathers of the North. This is the place of Rattling Hail Woman who holds the universe in her hands and teaches us that we must be consciously involved in the welfare of all.

Each of the directions may be thought of as a lodge. We must learn to be comfortable and to feel at home in each of the lodges. It is important that we do not avoid the teachings and lessons of one of the lodges, however difficult they might be for us. It is equally important that we don't become entrapped in the energy of any one of the lodges and never move away from it. Each has its dark side; the East spiritual pride and out-there spaciness; the South trap is the continual pain-games and sad stories we tell ourselves; the West is self-absorption and depression; the North arrogance and pedantry, knowledge without wisdom.

Each lodge serves as a mirror and is intended to show us what we need to know about ourselves in relation to the entire universe. The purpose of this is to help us return to the home of the True Self in the center of our own internal wheel of being.

Some people come in from the East and are full of inspired ideas and initiating energy. The next movement may be into the South, learning to play and enjoy life as a small child does. At this point people may be in love with the "light" and feel that to enter the darkness of the West, to face the unknown, is simply not in the interest of the New Age. They may feel all they need to do is say two million positive affirmations and everything that is difficult will pass. When you are a *puer* or *puella*, the archetypal eternal youth, enchanted with the light, it is most unsettling to look at the shadow side of things that dwell in the West. So these people will simply skip the West and move into the North. Here they may study many things and perhaps learn many spiritual disciplines, and gain much knowledge. Perhaps enough that they may even begin to teach others or become very successful in a particular line of work. But the knowledge will not be wisdom, as that can only be gained by looking deeply within and through the processing of life's experiences, no matter how painful or difficult. Until this is done their teaching will be hollow and the ego will become hard and impenetrable. Unless the inner realm is faced these people move back into the East and begin to project their own shadows that they have been too frightened to look at, onto everything and everyone that differs from them in even the slightest ways.

When they return to the South they will be ready to numb themselves with any and everything possible to avoid the shadows of self that have grown larger and more ominous as time has passed and they have been ignored.

And so the cycle goes, until the entire thing collapses, and a nervous breakdown, or a bout with alcohol or drugs has finally been lost, or spouse and family have deserted because one or more of the addictions has finally alienated them all. At this point, if the person is lucky, he or she will finally enter the West and begin the long overdue process of introspection and re-ensoulment.

Other people may enter life from the South in full childlike innocence, but may have experienced great abuse and neglect. When they move into the West they may become so self-absorbed with looking within that they become lost in the dark corridors of the psyche. This can result in extreme depression, obsessive narcissism, and inertia. Or if they move directly from the West to the East, skipping the give-away place of the North, they may move into a state of frenzied activity and find themselves on an endless seesaw ride of manic depression.

Others may originate in the place of the West and be inward and timid and may learn about the North through having and caring for children, which is, of course, an enormous give-away. These people may skip the lessons of the East and move into the South, which, without the inspiration of the East, may be a place of plodding attention to details and mundane activities, with no sense of purpose or excitement. Their lives will be dull and boring and they may feel themselves in an existential nightmare in which their lives have no purpose or meaning, especially after the children have left home and the spouse has run off with a younger and more exciting partner.

Other people may skip the South because the circumstances of their lives made their own early years so difficult that they never got to experience their own childhoods. These people may be filled with so much seriousness that they make all of life an enormous drudgery. They are often full of self-importance and totally lack the ability to laugh at themselves or at the world.

The Great Wheel is powerful as a tool to bring us to a deeper relationship with ourselves and it also connects us with a larger community that includes plants, animals, rivers, and solar systems. Everything has a place in the wheel, even infinity.

We have included a chart that lists some of the attributes of each of the directions. It is important to remember that it is a conceptual system and, like all conceptual systems, it is somewhat arbitrary and limited.

CHART OF THE DIRECTIONS

63
FINDING
YOUR
PLACE
IN THE
CIRCLE

	EAST	SOUTH	WEST	NORTH
Number	1	3	2	4
Element	Fire	Water	Earth	Wind
Color	Gold	Red	Black	White
Sound	He	Ha	Hu	Ho
Mineral	Yellow Sulfur	Rose Quartz, Coral	Smokey Quartz, Quartz	White Crystal
Season	Spring	Summer	Autumn	Winter
Time of Day	Sunrise	Noon	Sunset	Midnight
Weather	Sunny, Drought	Rain	Fog	Snow, Thunder, Lightning
Universe	Stars, Sun	Sacred Plants (Animals)	Planets, Earth	Sweet Medicine
Animal	Hawk, Eagle	Mouse, Coyote	Bear, Owl, Snake, Raven	Buffalo, Bighorn Sheep
Spirit of Animals	Winged ones	Swimmers	Crawlers	Four-Leggeds
Phase	Root, Seed	Beginning	Fruition	Give-away
Time	Future Time	Present Time	Out-of-Time	Past Time
Law	Cosmic	Natural	Magical	Civil
Human	Man	Child	Woman	Grandparents
Body Part	Genitals	Heart/Belly	Womb/Body	Mind
Center	Spirit	Heart	Soul	Logos
Expressing	Enthusiasm	Trust	Change	Love-of-Truth
Negative Emotions	Anger	Fear	Depression	Hysteria
Jungian Type	Intuition	Feeling	Sensate	Thinking
Mode/Gift	Vision, Inspiration	Innocence, Trust	Introspection	Wisdom, Knowledge
Attributes	Clarity	Love	Power, Beliefs	Wisdom
Life Cycles	Rebirth	Birth	Death	Maturation

Chart of the Directions—continued

	EAST	SOUTH	WEST	NORTH
Being	Fantasy, Imagination	Emotional	Dreams	Intellect
Ways of Knowing	Inner Vision, Clairvoyance	Feeling, Touch, Hearing	Inner Voice, Intuition	Prophesy, Pre-cognition
Role	Poet, Artist	Musician, Ceremo-nialist	Shaman	Chief, Teacher
Power	Illumination, Enlighten-ment	Trust, Inno-cence	Introspection, Intuition	Wisdom, Logic
Experience	Spiritual	Emotional	Physical	Mental
Mind	Conscious Mind, Lower Self, Ego-self	Collective Unconscious, Natural Mind	Subconscious, Deep Mind, Death Mind	Superconscious, Meditating Self, Big Mind
Warrior Aspects	Responsi-bility of Harmony	Attitude of Humility	Intent of Honor	Discipline of Humor
Enemies	Pride	Fear	Power	Arrogance
Challenges	Anxiety, Hysteria	Fear	Depression	Anger
Goddesses	Spider Woman	White Buffalo Woman	Beautiful Shell Woman, Changing Woman	Rattling Hail Woman Who Holds Up The Universe
Four Great Meanings	Protection	Nourishment	Growth	Wholeness
Sacred Object	Pipe	Drum	Rattle	Fan
Love	Love of Spirit	Erotic Love	Self-Love	Other-Love
Way to Be	To Will	To Dare	To Be Silent	To Know
Yoga	Karma Yoga	Bhakti Yoga	Hatha Yoga	Jhana Yoga
Winds	Breeze	Hot Wind	Cold Wind	Hard Wind
To Live Well	Speak Truth, Spirit Tongue	Pay Attention	Not Attached to Outcome	Show Up
Higher Purpose	Visionary	Healer	Teacher	Warrior

Chart of the Directions—continued

	EAST	SOUTH	WEST	NORTH
Meditation	Walking	Lying	Sitting	Standing
Instrument	Bell	Drum	Bones, Sticks	Rattle
Healing Salve	Singing for Your Life	Storytelling	Honoring of Silence	Dancing Your Life
Buddha Way	Right Placement	Right Speech	Right Timing	Right Action
Way	Authentic Knowing	Self-Conscious Self-Healing	Alright With The Unknown	Self Totally Present
Right Actions	Tell Truth With No Blame or Judgment	Forgiveness, Renewal, Regeneration	Breaking Patterns, Discernment	Good Modeling, Walking Your Talk

Different cultures have different ways of describing the energies of the directions. The European pagans and the western Cabalists have a system that is widely used in circling communities. In this system the East represents air, the South is fire, West is water, and North is earth.

Elizabeth Cogburn has developed a chant for each of the directions. For the East, "Image, dare, act"; the South, "Heart's desire, thy will be done"; the West, "Yes life"; and the North, "No attachments to our creations." She also includes the above and the below as directions with the chant "In essence we are all complete" for the above, and for the below, "Mysteries are sources of power and joy."

BUILDING A GREAT WHEEL OF LIFE

If you want to build a wheel outside, find a place that is quiet and protected. You may want to build it alone or with friends as a group ceremony. It can be built out of rocks that you or your friends have collected. You might want to use rocks that are beautiful and especially meaningful to you. The size of the wheel should be determined based on the area and the way you intend to use the wheel. Begin by smudging yourself and the others present, the area, and the rocks. First a rock is placed in the center, representing the Great Mystery. This is done with a prayer that invites Spirit to bless your wheel and declares your intention for the wheel. Then a rock is placed on the outer rim in each of the cardinal directions with prayers that call in those powers.

Then rocks are placed around the rim at each of the four midpoints. The following are some of the attributes of the midpoints:

Southeast: orange, great teachers and avatars, keepers of traditions, academic learning and teaching, the concept of self.

Here all the great teachers of the past sit, Buddha, Kwan Yin, Black Elk, White Buffalo Woman, Jesus, Mary Magdalene. Here are the keepers of the traditions that have grown out of human experience and wisdom. Here is the place where we hold all our concepts of self, both light and dark. It is here that we can find our selves in perfect balance.

Northeast: green, pure science, design of energy movement, old age, laws, morals.

Here is the place we learn to choreograph and direct our energy in relationship to self and to others. It is here we use our energy well or we waste and exhaust it, or we are lazy and listless. Here we either design and manifest success or we sabotage it. Here we make changes and express our selves with absolute impeccability. Here we give our emotions away, or hold them.

Northwest: brown, government and family, rules and laws, power, the circle of law, Karma, Karma Lords.

This is where we learn what we value, what our expectations are and what our boundaries are. Here we learn that what we sow we reap. It is here that we learn of our Sacred Truth and determine to defend it with honor. Here we learn how we limit ourselves and others with rigid ways and learn to align ourselves with the natural and cosmic rules and laws that govern life.

Southwest: turquoise, dreams, Sacred Dream, religion, Kachinas, symbols.

Here is where we dream and where we dance our Sacred Dream awake. This is the place of our symbols and metaphors. Here we learn which of our life symbols are closed and here we begin to open them. Here we both fear and long to examine ourselves. It is from here that we begin to fully extend ourselves into the dance that is life.

The next step is to build a smaller circle of eight rocks like the first one but only a few inches or feet from the center rock. Then you place rocks to create spokes that connect the inner hub with the outer rim. This is the design of the basic Wheel. More rocks can be placed on either rim or along the spokes any time there is a prayer to be made. Some people bury small crystals or sage, cornmeal or other special things under the rocks. All this is accompanied by smudging and you might want to end the process with singing or dancing.

Once built, this wheel can be used for personal or group meditation and ritual groups can meet around it. When you feel stuck in your life and are searching for direction you can go sit or walk around it and listen for the wisdom it can provide.

We know of people who live in city apartments without any outdoor space available who make small wheels with rocks glued on a plywood square, which they use for personal meditation or as the centerpiece for ceremonial circles. Others keep some beautifully polished rocks in a bag and use them to create a portable wheel wherever they are.

We have a very beautiful Wheel here on our dance ground. It is large and is made from desert rocks that questers have brought us from the personal wheels they have made to sit in during their last solo night.

THE VISION QUEST—A CIRCLE OF ONE

The vision quest is a time-honored way to find one's place in the Great Circle. Historically the vision quest, an important part of Native American life, was undertaken by individuals at important life-transitions such as puberty and changes in life purpose, as well as at times of group and personal crisis. Sometimes the purpose of the quest was to understand one's personal destiny and the path to be walked, and at other times it was to gain a vision for the survival of all the people.

The term is generic and anthropological rather than Native American, however. A form of vision questing has been done on every continent and in every culture. The Mediterranean nomads went on solo journeys as did the Australian aborigines. The knights searching for the Holy Grail were questing for vision and wisdom. In India and China seekers would spend solitary time in caves sitting for enlightenment.

Contemporary questers have in common a desire to find their places in the wheels of their lives and to open to the powers of nature, silence, and prayer.

Several times a year I, Sedonia, take small groups of people into the magnificent landscape of the southern California desert on a quest for vision and power. By power I mean the strength and wisdom that each of us has gained through life experience; it is our *real* power. To gain this power is to process and find the power in our life experience that enables us to stop seeing ourselves as victims. It requires that we own all the parts of ourselves, not just the light, clean, and acceptable. It means learning the lessons of our wounds. It is the very best of us and is what we have to share with the world, and the quest to find it is an aspect of every spiritual path.

The most immediate experience of the desert is one of expansion and grandeur with majestic mountains on all sides, incredible sunrises and

Questers circle in prayer and mindfulness as they prepare to pass through a major severance threshold on their way to the desert.

sunsets, a blanket of stars in the night sky, endless variations of design on the sandy desert floor. Upon close examination the abundance of life is evident: tiny delicate plants and flowers, small mice, rattlesnakes, lizards, coyotes, foxes, moths, all blending into the stillness. In each mountain surrounding the desert valley a different colored mineral predominates. All the mountains have gifted the desert floor with limitless varieties of rocks. In the sunlight it seems like a tray of jewels. The desert floor is a labyrinth of washes making it impossible to walk in a straight line, forcing

A group of vision questers holding hands in a prayer circle in the desert.

one into thinking of space and movement in a more feminine, less linear way.

The first few days of the ten-day journey are spent in intense preparation, clarifying intentions, acknowledging fears, learning about desert safety and respect, sharing teaching, all this while sitting in circle. During this time, as we leave civilized comfort and familiar habits, the transitions that mark our severance from the small round of our daily lives are acknowledged.

The day arrives for the questers to leave base camp and go to the spot on the mountain that has called them, thus crossing the threshold, entering the sacred time and place of The Great Round. Now they are in the realm of Spirit. For three days and nights they will stay on the mountain alone, fasting, singing, praying, opening to Spirit.

The third day on the mountain is devoted to building a circle of stones, each quester's Great Wheel. In this wheel each stone is placed to represent something or someone that has a powerful personal meaning to the quester: a relationship, an aspect of the culture, an emotion, a place, a problem, a fear. The questers are asked to face the things they feel negative about and embrace the things they feel positive about. Having a balance of positive and negative stones creates the tension that energizes the power

Dolores LaChapelle creating a circle of one as she does T'ai Chi on a
mountain ledge. *Photo: Steve Meyers*

of the wheel. The purpose of this wheel of stones is to integrate all these
parts into a whole. The whole is the Self of the individual. The teaching
is that *we are the Wheel.*

The last night the quester stays awake inside the wheel, sometimes
dancing or singing, crying for a vision. During this time Spirit comes in
many forms. Sometimes the wind whispers, sometimes the stars speak,
animals appear as totems, rocks teach. The more humble and silent one
becomes, the more receptive one is to the teachings of the Great Spirit.

During that last night the solitary quester, experiencing how small and
vulnerable she or he is in relationship to the powers of the Universe, also
finds a place within that is much larger and more expansive than she or
he had ever imagined. This experience of sitting in one's solitary circle of
power, finding one's place in the great web of life, brings one into an

experience and acceptance of the totality of Self. Once the Great Wheel is integrated into the questers they bring it back into all their circles and become more effective members of the community, carrying a deep understanding that they are in the right place, that they are at home on this earth and that they have important work to do.

Vision quests are one very powerful and time-proven way of moving an individual beyond the personal concerns of the small round of daily life and into the Great Round of global awareness and action, into a vision that is large enough to contain all of life, and into a commitment to that vision.

The people who choose to make these journeys come from many walks of life and many directions. In many ways they are ordinary people but in their courage and commitment to discover the truth at the center of their beings they are extraordinary. They are each willing to undergo the discomforts and trials of desert survival, devoid of most comforts, to be dirty and sweaty, sometimes hot, sometimes cold, to eat small and simple meals and to fast from food for three days and nights, to sit on the rocky desert floor, and for one night to do without sleep. They are willing to move into the unknown and to confront their fears of the tonal and of the nagual, the outer and the inner. They are willing to make themselves vulnerable to nature, to one another, and to Spirit. Most importantly, they are willing to take on their power and all the responsibilities that go with it.

FIVE

BEING IN CIRCLE

Sometimes I go about pitying myself,
and all the time
I am being carried by great winds across the sky.
Ojibwe adapted by ROBERT BLY

The technologies of circle making facilitate the creation of a safe container, the weaving of a ceremonial basket. The container becomes the setting and context for the real, deep transformative work. The circle process encourages its participants to move more fully into authentic being and to develop a vision for their lives.

Being is *Being* in present time, totally in the moment, as fully present with all our parts as we can be. Present time is sacred time. In the deepest part of ourselves we all want to live in the present because there we are most alive, most connected. When we do not honor the reality of this, our physical bodies get locked in somatic patterns of fear caused by the holding of other, unresolved experiences. This conflict is felt both in the psyche and in our cells and tissues, and it prevents the pulsating aliveness of the moment. Yet in each moment the redemption of awareness is possible, in each moment we are given the opportunity to let go of fear and to allow ourselves to give and receive love.

Invoking, drumming, smudging, all bring on thresholds of experience that sever us from the conditioned, habitual world and guide us into a state of liminality. The liminal state is a transpersonal condition in which we are between the worlds and not attached to our worldly identity. The freedom in this state is a feeling of co-creating with Spirit and offers us the opportunity to make and define ourselves any way we want. There is

73

an experience of expanded identity, but it is not the ego that grows, it is the feeling of oneness, offering us the opportunity for transformation and healing.

THE AUTHENTIC SELF AND THE WITNESS

Angeles Arrien says that we need to do four things to make our lives work and they apply to being authentic in the circle as well. She says we must show up, pay attention, tell the truth, and not be attached to the outcome.

A circling community allows many opportunities to practice these skills by teaching us to be fully present, to pay attention to our deepest impulses, and to be alert and aware of others. We learn to tell the truth so that we can be deeply known just as we are while discovering more about ourselves. Our commitment needs to be so great to these principles that we will do them regardless of the outcome. This means that we "give-away" from the very best of ourselves. What makes a circle safe for practicing this radically authentic behavior, for going through public transformation, is the unique quality that arises when there is harmony between the personal and transpersonal.

This state of awareness, contained within a circle, generates an energy that cannot come from any other place. This is what has been called in many traditions "The Witness." To be an effective witness requires that we pay attention, not project, interpret, judge, or try to "fix" the other. There is no room for interference in another's process. The witness is asked to sit in his or her own circle of power, pay attention, take responsibility for what he or she is feeling, and not project his or her experience onto the other. The only way to really see someone else is to fully own our emotions, feelings, and thoughts.

The need to be really seen is as great as the need for food and shelter, yet most of us go through life starving for reflection. We all need to be seen with eyes filled with love, acceptance, and adoration. There is a terrible loneliness and alienation when we feel no one sees, hears, or understands us. This loneliness lingers in circles unless the quality of witnessing is present.

Sometimes, as part of witnessing, people go through a stage in which they seem to know what they are feeling and they take the certainty that affords them and assume they know what others are feeling. This is not witnessing. For instance, sometimes when people feel afraid of another's pain they will immediately reach out to hug or stroke them, which stops the process, or they might come up with a solution to the other person's dilemma or discount the other's feelings by saying it's not really so bad.

All these are the reactions of someone who is afraid of his or her own pain, of someone who is not being in circle.

Learning how to witness is essential because we live in a time when great numbers of people are beginning to tell their truths. Some of these truths are hard to hear, some involve terrible childhood abuse and betrayal, yet they must be told and heard. When they are not heard properly the telling is undermined and damage, rather than healing, may result. It can take a long time to regain the courage to tell the story again.

In the circle process, when people sit and speak from the deepest part of themselves, no matter how wounded, how much anguish or how many tears, they, at that moment, are sitting in their circle of power. They need to be witnessed, that is, to be respected for their willingness to go so deep and be so vulnerable. What is required of us as witnesses is to sit in our own circle of power, owning our own pain and fear, fully being with those feelings and not projecting them outward.

Our stories need to be heard, not fixed. Nobody needs fixing, we are not machines. All we need is to be heard. We need someone else to know how hard it was, to know that we have survived with dignity and that we are not afraid to feel. We as human beings need more than anything else to be seen, known, felt, accepted, and loved.

When people are real in the circle we love them for their process of becoming whole. We love each other for being who we are, with all our perfections and imperfections. The essence of the process is to validate that we are living, breathing, dancing, real people, who feel pain and fear and make mistakes, while loving and caring about each other. The circle form creates a place for everyone to work, pray, be real, and feel at one with each other, all together.

Being in a circle teaches us to respect ourselves and one another. When this happens we are brought into an experience of immanence and sacredness, making us better able to honor the beauty and integrity of the earth. If enough people gather in circle and grapple with their identities within this context, it enhances the possibilities for us all. Creative group dynamic is essential if we are going to mobilize healing and create an ecological environment for ourselves.

THE INNER FAMILY

Inside each of us there is an inner family, or council of four, composed of an adult woman and man, a little girl and a little boy. For an individual to be healthy and whole each inner family member needs to be known, respected, and heard. This is difficult because most of us carry within us residues of childhood repression. Adult tyranny has affected the child within us all and seldom has the loving potential between parents and children been met. Most of us bring neglect and shame-based pain into the circle.

The little boy inside men, and the little girl inside women, usually carry the childhood wounding. When these children don't feel safe they can bring a lot of disruption to an individual's life and can wreak havoc in a circle. Their fear can easily turn into controlling behavior and can cause the person to feel he or she has to either leave the group or, if he or she stays with the circle, to disrupt and undermine it.

The needs of our inner, same-gender child need to be met by our inner adults. When we learn to really listen and nurture this needy child within ourselves we don't need other people to do it for us. We become our own mother and father and quit looking for parenting outside ourselves.

The opposite-gender child, that is, the little girl in men and the little boy in women, is called the spirit child and is usually the source of creation and playfulness, freedom and spirit connection. When the wounded child is allowed to run the show the spirit child often disengages and leaves and the individual and the circle are deprived of its gifts.

When the inner woman and man become friends and allies, cooperating with, encouraging and respecting one another, and give loving attention to the little wounded child within, there is space for the inner spirit child to really shine and bring magic into our lives. Then we can express the joyfulness and celebration of life that we came here to experience.

▌NNER-FAMILY CEREMONY

This is a technique for getting in touch with the inner family. Find four small rocks that seem special to you. After you have smudged yourself, the area, and the rocks, place them in the four directions on a nice cloth in front of you. You should sit facing the north. The rock in the south represents your same-gender little child, the rock in the west your opposite-gender adult, the rock in the north your same-gender adult and the rock in the east your opposite-gender spirit child.

You can begin with any rock. Hold it in your left hand, next to your belly, and begin to ask it questions about the part of yourself it represents. Ask what joys are there, what pains and sorrows. Ask if it feels part of the family or separate; if it feels heard, respected, appreciated; what it needs from the other inner-family members; what would make it feel safe and protected; what gives it pleasure and whether it gets enough of it; whether its needs are met or ignored. Work with each of the four rocks in this way until each family member has been heard. You can hold two rocks and find ways that the parts they represent can communicate and relate better.

Sometimes this ceremony will be the first time that parts of the inner family have ever known that the others exist, much less cooperated with one another. Your inner family is a circle and no one member of that inner circle should have the ability to tyrannize the others. Each one's voice should be respected and honored, just as in any circle. Your sense of "I" should be able to move around and give voice to each of the parts inside you at any time it is appropriate.

When you have received all the information you need for the moment, thank the rocks and place them either on your altar or in a special pouch or bag. You can return to them any time you wish and repeat the ceremony. You will gradually come to know these parts of yourself very well and become more and more responsive to their needs. As you do this you will become more whole and integrated, better able to love and care for yourself and better able to be with others in a full and open manner. Your ability to be in a circle will be enhanced and expanded.

In a circle there should be room for our hurt and needy children to show themselves but they shouldn't be allowed to manipulate the group process. The better each individual can care for her or his own inner child the easier it will be to expose that vulnerable part and have it witnessed by others, which increases the healing for all present. Each time we circle it is possible to experience an integration of the many parts of our self.

ENTERING AND LEAVING A CIRCLE

Being in a well-functioning circle will help bring you into harmony with a group of people, an extended family. In the beginning you might have to grapple with feelings of shyness and fear. This is not unusual; many people feel that way. It is really better to be honest about this rather than trying to convince people that it is otherwise. Most people have a lot of compassion when someone will just plainly say he or she is afraid or shy.

Entering an already functioning circle can produce an anxiety that can be very discouraging for beginners. If you find yourself in this position give yourself permission to just sit quietly, without having to know what is going to happen or what you are going to do. You can become more active as you gain confidence. Give yourself permission to be in the space of not-knowing for as long as it takes.

To prepare yourself for being in a circle pause briefly and take a few full breaths into your belly. Do this for a few seconds or minutes. This makes room for your actions and words to come from a centered place. When your level of truth is responded to, when the people with you acknowledge the brilliance that is your birthright, it increases the level of personal blessings for all present. What comes from the belly is intuitive, wise, and interesting. Elizabeth Cogburn calls this belly-breath of interconnectedness the "shaman's pause." It is a method of responding rather than reacting.

Each time we sit in a circle we gain the experience and confidence to respond to everyday situations creatively. We practice ways of being in the circle, not only for the tremendous benefits at that moment, but also to bring them into our daily lives. An effective circle allows us to bring the teachings into everyday reality. Each time we sit in a circle it allows a deeper experience of our own and one another's authenticity and heightens our commitment to creating a world in which that is the normal way to be. One of the unique values of the ceremonial circle in comparison to solitary spiritual disciplines and paths is that the teaching has to do with being related, with being in an egalitarian community.

Culturally we have taken individualism about as far as it can go. Most of us have experienced deeply ingrained feelings of isolation and alienation. It takes time and patience to grow past this conditioning and when things become challenging or difficult in a circle it is tempting to retreat back into protective isolation. Some people leave the circle at this point and invest their fearful energy into relationships or habit patterns that are less challenging and that don't nudge them to consciousness.

There is a legitimate time to question and feel whether the circle provides a safe enough place for you to take the kinds of risks that are necessary and inherent in the process of personal transformation.

It is perfectly natural to want to flee when you come up against a deeply unraveling psychological experience that demands an expanded sense of selfhood. Fear can come up in subtle ways. People find all sorts of reasons to leave a circle, running when things get too real or scary, and will find many ways to rationalize their behavior. They might not like one small aspect of the circle and magnify it out of all proportion, or they might decide that everyone in the circle is wrong, rather than admitting their own fear. When someone does this and resolution or closure is not provided, it can leave a huge energy leak in the circle that will have to be mended and healed.

One way to avoid this is to discuss the possibility beforehand and to make an agreement to have a closure ceremony should anyone decide to leave. Sometimes, if a person is really upset, he or she will refuse to keep this agreement, and then the circle will have to find a way to mend itself. For instance, the person who has left abruptly can be symbolically placed in the center of the circle and everyone can speak to him or her, sharing anger, distress, as well as feelings of goodwill. This should continue until everyone in the circle finds the generosity within themselves to release the person with blessings.

A good circle should have space for you to create the conditions you need for safety. When a circle becomes a well-woven basket, with no place for energy to leak, it becomes a truly safe container where each member can do unsafe things; that is, go through deep revealing and transformation, with the circle as witness. When a circle is committed to this level of work an agreement may be made among members that all the things that have been shared in the circle will be held as sacred and not revealed to others outside the circle. When individuals leave a circle for any reason they should be able to assure the remaining members that this agreement of silence will be honored and that members' secrets will remain within the group.

When couples belong to the same circle it can sometimes cause a problem if one decides to leave the circle. Either member of a couple should be able to decide independently whether to leave or join a circle. Often it is healthy for couples to have separate circles so they can receive part of their nurturance and sense of self from sources outside the relationship. The gifts gained separately in circle should enrich the individual and the relationship should prosper from the experience.

Feeling part of a circle can bring an incredible exhilaration as one identifies one's self with the collective "I." An actual living entity inside is suddenly able to speak truth and move past limitations of personality into the broad and expansive field of self. At this point there might arise a feeling of deep impatience with the necessarily slow and organic development of a well-functioning circle. The challenge is to continually learn how to go deeper, to keep learning through experience, to get closer and closer to the authentic voice and listener, to the real story. The richness of the process is found where learning is shared in dialogue with friends.

THE CIRCLE FAMILY

In a very real sense the circle provides a spiritual family with whom to practice reality. Nothing is as revitalizing to the soul as to suddenly awaken to the fact that the solitary phase of spiritual practice is over and there are friends with whom to walk the path. A cohesive group of people resonating from the depths of their beings generates a quality of experience that really feels like being in a family. To get to the root of self one has to pass through personal reflection and end up safe in the arms of many friends.

Being in circle with others is a process of allowing them into our lives, so it is very important to be discriminating. Often when people really join forces they will do so on all levels, including the economic and moral. You really have to be able to trust that the people you are with say what they mean and mean what they say; that they don't say anything about you to others that they wouldn't say to you; that they are committed to work on their personal issues so that their unconscious and addictive places don't create sinkholes for the entire group.

This last point is very important. It is very common for groups to get sidetracked responding to the continual distress of one or more of the members. While this may seem like a compassionate use of the group's energy it often is not, and it would be better for the distressed members to resolve their issues in a special session of the circle, or in a more traditional therapeutic situation. One or two disturbed people can sabotage an entire circle if the participants don't know how to respond to them.

If this happens in a circle you are part of and you are unable to redirect the focus it may be necessary to leave the circle. In this way circles are somewhat like marriages. They deserve a working-it-out period, but sometimes you simply have to acknowledge that it's not right and leave to be true to your authentic self. You can then create or join a circle that is more suited to your needs and wishes.

In a real circle it feels like deep connection is flowing between all the members, but it is also natural to feel closer to some than others, to even have strong attractions to certain people. It is important not to become confused about the communal impulse by acting it out sexually. So many efforts at building community have been undermined when members went for the short-term, feel-good experience of the moment and were not ready to grapple with the deeper levels of identity that get activated by being in vital contact with other people.

Coyote

The coyote is the trickster who teaches us to laugh at ourselves, especially when we are taking ourselves too seriously, or when we imagine ourselves to be too precious and special. The coyote mimics our pretensions and is a necessary force in the circle. You will notice coyote's presence when, for instance, at a very sacred moment, as you step forward to light the candles and invoke the Spirit powers, none of the candles will stay lit. Coyote often comes when one is particularly interested in doing something correctly and properly, and needing to make a good impression.

Some people are innately inclined to embody the coyote spirit and there should be a place in the circle for them to express this perspective. It helps keep everyone more clear and balanced.

There are also people who are disruptive and bring confusion to a circle that is caused by their unhealed and frightened inner child. They might want to identify this as coyote but it is not.

When we are in the desert, vision questing, spirit coyote often comes to test the intention and determination of the questers. Spirit coyote will whisper things in their ears, telling them that we have packed up base camp and left the desert, deserting them, or perhaps that they should go down the mountain, hitchhike into town for a milkshake and fries, and no one would ever know the difference. Once coyote was audacious enough to tell a quester that we were making ice cream at base camp (in 98° weather) and we were calling the questers back to share it with them. Fortunately these questers knew how to deal with a coyote. To deal with him you look him right in the eye and say "I see you coyote, what do you want?" Coyote has to tell the truth then, which is that all he really wants is for them to get stronger and clearer within themselves and in their intentions. Coyote is an ally, wanting us always to succeed, testing us and pushing us all the while.

Coyote can come to us inside a circle, or in our day-to-day lives, in this same way. His whisperings that seem so mocking, causing all our doubts to arise, are simply intended to bring us closer to our true path. It is easy to imagine his laughter when he has tricked us, and his pride and delight in us when we refuse to be tricked.

There are many strata of experience that are passed through as one learns to feel empowered by real participation in the circle-making process. It takes time and there are palpable changes at each turn in the road. Learning how to be with people is a long, long process. Authentic being brings the self into a vast, interconnected oneness that includes much unknown territory. From being in circles a state of selfhood emerges that can reconcile all of the relationships we enter. In this way the circle serves us as we venture into that realm where we are related on an even deeper level than blood.

The circle process allows us to work psychologically, in a transpersonal context, while building a community. Establishing a cohesive circle is an integral part of re-inhabiting the earth. While weaving personal connections and ties, we also explore the inner world. The personal being becomes part of a larger context. Being in circle provides the safety for us to stop identifying with the past so that we can feel the pulse of the present and, in this way, establish a future.

SIX

CIRCLING FOR THE EARTH

TEACHERS OF THE CIRCLE WAY

. . . the earth does not belong to us,
we belong to it.
BLACK ELK

People all over the earth have sat in circle together since the beginning of human culture. They learned how to be in circle together from the matrix of their culture. People were not designated as teachers of the circle, yet there was a viable transmission of circling knowledge. The current wave of circling has grown from the women's movement, and most specifically that part of the movement that is involved with women's spirituality. The issue of sharing power is integral to feminist thinking and the use of the circle has naturally and organically grown from that central issue.

We have chosen to include the words of eight women whose work we admire. Their work and words have taught and inspired us and they are very respected within their circling communities. They represent a variety of approaches to circling and community building. Each has a clear vision and a dedication to that vision, each circles for the earth.

The women we have interviewed come from a variety of backgrounds and have received inspiration in their work from various sources, Native American, European Paganism and Goddess traditions, the cabala, and the Chinese Tao, and all have been influenced by the best in Western psychology.

There are many others in the field whose work we respect but were not able to include. The field is growing and more and more people are being drawn to this form, some as teachers, many as participants in the small circling communities that are springing up everywhere.

STARHAWK

I met with Starhawk in her house in San Francisco. She had made time for me in the midst of her busy schedule, which included moving from one home to another. When I arrived she was being interviewed by *High Times* magazine, a periodical devoted to exploring and understanding the use of psychedelic drugs. When asked about the use of such sacraments during ritual and ceremony she was adamant that she did not encourage or condone the use of psychedelics in her circles.

Starhawk is the author of *The Spiral Dance, Dreaming the Dark*, and *Truth or Dare*. Her ability to communicate the processes of circling has resonated with people all over the world. She has integrated the ancient voice of European paganism with astute contemporary analysis of our political reality. Starhawk calls herself a witch as a way of reclaiming those European pagan shamans who were so brutally destroyed during the Inquisition.

One gets the feeling from being with Starhawk that one is with someone who is living an authentic existence. Besides being a ceremonialist, a writer, a therapist, and a teacher, Starhawk has been meeting with a circle of peers for a number of years where she is not the leader. Circling is a part of her personal life as well as her public one. Her style of teaching is one that is truly empowering to all present.

Reclaiming Community

CEREMONIAL CIRCLE: Let's talk about your work with circles.

Starhawk: There really isn't much you can do in life alone, certainly not if your goal is to make changes in the world. In order to do that you need to get together with other people. A small-group circle is the most effective way. It's the pattern that works best because it's somewhere in between the individual and the mass. In a small group you can connect intimately and be very strongly bonded, you can build community and it's still small enough that you can really know each other and at the same time become more aware as an individual.

CEREMONIAL CIRCLE: How do you see the creation of circles as a way of forming a larger community?

Starhawk: Small circles build up a network into larger groups and larger circles, and it's also a way of preserving diversity and some sort of unity, an ability to act together.

CEREMONIAL CIRCLE: Do you see circles having an effect toward social change?

Starhawk: Yes. To me, social change in this country has to be involved with cultural change. Some real challenges need to be made to the basic values that this country is run on. We have to change the way power is shared in relationships. Most of our values are based on a model of power that says the earth is made up of dead parts, that nature is not inherently valuable, and human beings are not valuable except as they can be used or exploited or meet certain criteria. All of these values come out of a world view that I call estrangement, which has contributed to us being in this situation in which we're destroying the ecology of the world, where we have an economic system that really hurts people, especially women and people of color, and where we stand a good chance of blowing up the world. There has to be political change in the most ordinary sense and there also has to be a change in consciousness. Consciousness is certainly individual, but not as individual as we think it is. I think consciousness is changed at the community level. Consciousness is very linked in with the community we live in, so if we really want to change consciousness we've got to do it within a group.

CEREMONIAL CIRCLE: It would seem that the very act of sitting in a circle requires a change in consciousness because of the structure.

Starhawk: Well, it is very different if you think about people sitting in a circle. First of all a circle has no head and no tail. Everyone is equal in a circle, everyone in a circle can see everybody else. Attention and energy can move from one person to another very fluidly, and if I say something brilliant everyone can look at me, and if someone else says something brilliant, everyone can look at that person. The energy can continually move and be passed around. In a lecture hall, when you have one person at the front, the energy focuses on that one person, the expert, the authority, the one who is giving us the word. When the other people say something or ask questions and you're sitting in the back, all you see is the backs of their heads. It's much harder for the energy to move.

CEREMONIAL CIRCLE: Could you speak a little about how you first got involved with this?

Starhawk: I first got involved with witchcraft when I was in college, back in the late sixties. What really appealed to me about it was that, first of all, it was a religion with a female image of the goddess and, also, that the sacred is the earth, this world here. It is the body, sexuality. It's where we actually are right now. Also it was based on small groups, on covens. Of course, covens take different forms and have different kinds of leadership but there was certainly the potential within it for me to be a leader, which I didn't feel in any of the mainstream religions, and also for a group to not have a leader but be collectively based on egalitarian principles. So I got involved a bit, drifted away, got very involved in the feminist movement and, in the mid-seventies, found that feminism and witchcraft came together in a feminist spirituality. It just seemed natural to me that the feminist movement should have some connection with a religon centered around the goddess.

CEREMONIAL CIRCLE: So, when did you first begin to organize circles?

Starhawk: I began when I moved to San Francisco in 1975. Later I started a women's coven. The original group was going through a lot of changes with the original people. New people came in and old people left. At that time we were still working more with the old model of having a high priestess, someone who was taking charge of the group, which would rotate and pass around. I had passed it on to someone else. That coven is still continuing. I think it is now in its third or fourth generation, completely composed of people I've never met. Then my friend Diane and I decided that we wanted to teach a class. We found that our group had gone through power struggles for years and had finally come to a place where we felt that there was a balanced flow of power in the group, and we wanted to teach in a way that could convey that from the beginning so that groups wouldn't have to go through the same kinds of struggle that we had. So we started teaching a class together, to co-teach a model of power. The class was structured so that people in the class took on responsibility and learned different parts of the ritual throughout the course. The women who took it were so excited that they wanted to go on and have another class. Before we knew it, we brought the rest of our coven into teaching and we had a collective.

At first, it really was just our coven. That was in 1980. Then in 1981 a number of us got involved with the Diablo campaign and went down to the blockade. At the same time we were planning a big public ritual, The Spiral Dance, for Halloween. Since we left in September, other people stepped in and took over the organizing of it. By the time the Spiral Dance was over, those people had come together and formed a larger, more expanded collective. That really was the nucleus of "Reclaiming," which is the name of the group. Reclaiming is an ongoing collective that still does classes, workshops, public rituals and publishes a newsletter.

CEREMONIAL CIRCLE: I'm interested in political action and how that grew out of the circle.

Starhawk: We felt that we should take part in it, that we should do direct action, blockade, and go to jail. That came directly out of our belief that the earth is sacred and that we had to do something to protect it. What we found was that the antinuclear organization, the Abalone Alliance, was organized on principles very close to ours. It was a larger network composed of small groups called affinity groups that were strongly bonded, that worked by consensus, that were egalitarian, that had no leaders. Every decision that was made for the organization was made by the affinity groups in a spokescouncil, so there was no top-down leadership or hierarchy. Everything was decided in such a way so that everyone in that group could have a voice in that decision. That was very important to us and very powerful. They also had a kind of process of consensus in their decision making that was more formalized and structured than any that we had used and we found that helpful.

We found in Reclaiming that we modified our structure to work in ways that were better for us so we made smaller work groups. We called them cells as a joke but the name stuck and so that's what they've been called ever since. They take on certain functions. There's a teacher cell that teaches classes and meets to discuss the teaching and the scheduling, there's a newsletter cell that puts out the newsletter. The whole collective meets at different times. It has met once a month, and at times it hasn't met for six months. For a while we were regularly meeting eight times a year. It varies according to need. As other projects come, a new cell will form to take them on.

In the beginning the collective was open like the Abalone Alliance structure, where anyone could come in and be a part of it if they wanted to. We found after a couple of years of working together that it didn't work for us at all because we were really involved in building community. We needed to know who we were building it with, who was going to be there for continuity. We also needed some sense of safety about who was going to be in our group, our process, and the relationships that we had formed over the years. We needed boundaries so we closed the collective. But we never have really figured out who is and who isn't in it. There's always people in a grey area on their way in or on their way out, and some people who are definitely in or definitely out. We have a sort of semipermeable membrane.

CEREMONIAL CIRCLE: What would you say if you were going to give people advice about starting a circle—how to start coming together to form a community?

Starhawk: The first thing I would say is, "just do it." Don't worry about whether or not you have the right or authority or know enough to do it. If you know what kind of group you want you just have to put it out and people will come along who want similar things. Together you can figure out how to do it. You may not know how to do ritual but there are resources around. Read some books. Make some things up. Try some things out and see what works and what doesn't work. Do something that feels good to you.

After long, hard, painful years of experience in groups, I've found the most important thing in really getting a group to work together is for people to be honest with each other. It sounds so simple it's almost ridiculous, but it is also the hardest thing to do in a group. If you can be open and honest about what you're feeling, you've got half of it solved, but that isn't generally what happens. Usually people have a lot of ideas in their heads about what we can and can't say, about what we can or can't think, and we try to be nice.

The third thing is that not everybody belongs in every group. I think if you really want to have community you should at least start off with people that you like to be around. That again seems so simple that it almost is ridiculous to say it but I've been in many groups where you sort of start off with the group open and there's someone in it that you really don't like. You feel like you shouldn't say anything, you know this is supposed to be a healing circle and how can I say anyone should not be a member? Sometimes it can go on for years, struggling and struggling to put people together who maybe have very different ideas about what they want.

I've been trying to identify what it is that makes certain groups healing situations as opposed to destructive situations. One of them is the idea of value. Everyone in a group has value just by virtue of being who they are, not by virtue of meeting certain standards, like being good. For example, in the Alcoholics Anonymous Twelve-step program, all you have to do is walk in the door. All you have to be is an alcoholic who wants to stop drinking. You don't have to stop drinking. You can backslide a million times and the group is still open to you.

Some of the ways that people get a sense of value is through structures that allow you to see and know each other, to tell your stories, talk about who you are, name each other, affirm each other in ritual, care for each other. Again, this doesn't necessarily mean that you are going to end up liking everyone. Sometimes it's less painful in the long run to say you have a value as a human being but I may not want to work in a group with you.

The other thing that is important in a group is safety. A lot of times people think about safety as "You're not going to get your feelings hurt" or "People are going to be nice to you." But safety is not really about that because in any group you will get your feelings hurt, if people are honest. Safety is about being able to share risks, so that if anyone is asking one person to take a risk, it's a risk that you all take. If we're going to sit here and I'm going to talk to you about my experiences, I know you are also going to talk about similar experiences. You're not sitting there to judge me. That's why I think support groups are so effective when people share the same kinds of experience, because then we share the same risk in telling them.

Safety also involves having a sense of boundaries, knowing who is in it and who is not in it, or knowing at least what are the purposes and what are the conditions for being there. In AA, it is wide open, anyone can walk in off the street, their meetings aren't closed but there's a real clear boundary in "This is the purpose of the group, to help people stop drinking." It's not to overthrow the government and it's not to help you make more money, etc. Safety is about things being out in the open. There always are power struggles, gossip, conflicts, sexual liaisons. All that stuff is always going on in every group, even if it's only in fantasy, and when it is out in the open it's not so hard to deal with. When it's hidden people feel very unsafe. Something related to that is a ritual of breaking silence about things, coming out with what has been hidden and secret. That's why incest support groups or AA or consciousness-raising groups are so powerful. They allow you to say what has always been un-sayable.

For a group to really be empowering in the long run, it has to be sustainable. In an ecological sense, you have to get as much energy back from it as you put into it. That may, in very concrete terms, mean that in order to sustain a group for a long time, some people get paid for some of the work because that will replace some of the energy they would otherwise have to put into earning a living. It might mean that people need appreciation for some of their work, or that the work needs to be shared, or that the group needs to take on doing less. Every group needs to look at that question, "How are we going to balance the energy?"

CEREMONIAL CIRCLE: In closing I would like a visionary statement. What is the best future we could imagine?

Starhawk: I guess the best future I could imagine is a world or society where we have a different kind of balance structure; that allows for many more different varieties of ways to live and relationships to have; where many more people live in collective households, rather than all the little single family boxes; where children would be raised with many people involved in their care; where at the same time there is room for people who would rather live by themselves, who need more privacy and space; where there's a real kind of experimental, fluid, rich diversity of ways to live; where, when you go to work, instead of having a hierarchical relationship with a boss, the work is done in small groups and collectives; where everyone who works has a real voice in how that work is structured, how it's marketed, how it is priced, who buys it, who gets it; where the resources come from and the conditions under which things are produced and made, what its purpose is; where the work you do is something that is meeting people's needs in some real way and not contributing to more and more destruction; and where people live in larger communities that have some kind of base of celebration together, in neighborhoods and cities where people are knit together with common celebrations that become rituals, through common experiences, through common aspects of their day-to-day life, so that the fabric of the community itself creates a safe environment for children, for old people, for everybody; where people are looking out for each other.

CEREMONIAL CIRCLE: Thanks. That's a real good one.

ANTHEA FRANCINE

I met with Anthea in her small cottage on a quiet street in Berkeley. She is a tall and striking woman who was born in England and speaks with a lovely accent. She welcomed me graciously and the entire interview had a warmth and flow about it that was very pleasing.

We met in her office, a bright and sunny loft that was the most special spot in her house, making me think that here is a woman who takes herself and her work seriously.

Anthea has an M.A., which she received from the Theological Union in Berkeley, with an emphasis on the feminine dimension of the Divine. She is a workshop leader and ceremonialist and was a cofounder of Women's Quest, a network of circles for the exploration and practice of women's spirituality. She has a private counseling practice, which she refers to as "soul work." She has worked internationally leading workshops on life-story as sacred myth and life as sacred art. She is a consultant to businesses and health-care groups, working toward models that would include the feminine perspective. She has a deep concern for peace issues and carries an exciting vision of the Goddess rising to dance.

Circles Are the Cells of the Goddess

CEREMONIAL CIRCLE: Why do you use the circle in your work?

Anthea: To me the circle is the mandala. A mandala is a geometric image with concentric counterbalanced components that emerge from the imagination of the individual as a symbol of wholeness and integration.

Every moment is a mandala. If you think of yourself as an eye of awareness standing in the middle of the entire universe, at all moments, everything radiates out from you as a point of awareness, then you are an axis mundi. You are a kind of lightning conductor for the consciousness of the divinity as you stand in the middle of your circle. We can't help being in a circle.

There is a 360-degree reality around us at all moments. We've been taught to look in straight lines. That means we look at one degree and let the other 359 degrees of reality just disappear. That's tunnel vision, which is linear, ego, and mental vision. It's an okay kind of vision if you want to get certain jobs done, but in terms of spirituality, which has to be holistic, it's a different matter.

When we sit in a circle it reminds us that the point of reference is the middle, and the middle is both empty and full of everything. Everyone is equidistant from the middle so there is no sense of hierarchy. The point of reference changes as different people speak. It is a different kind of focusing and a different type of awareness about relationship to one another and to the whole when we sit in a circle.

When we get out of our minds and stop talking about what the five-year plan looks like, and get into our hearts and act in the moment out of the synchronicity, serendipity, and grace of the moment, we are in harmony. Then the vision will fulfill itself. We do not have to know what it is. I think we often make the mistake of feeling we need to know what we are doing. We only need to know what we are doing ourselves and what is or isn't working now. If I have a problem with you now and we resolve it, then our part of the tapestry is okay. And if you go away and do that in every moment of your day and so do I, then our individual threads of the tapestry are intact. As each of us does that work, so the weaving will weave, because the Goddess is doing the weaving. I'm not responsible for the whole weaving. I'm only responsible for my thread, for my piece, and the key for my piece is Radical Authenticity. When I am totally authentic at all times I have taken care of my business and my business is all I can take care of.

The circle is a cell. There are millions and millions of cells in the body of the Goddess. The cellular form is one that allows movement. A flux of components can come and go according to what the Goddess is doing as she is weaving this thing together. I trust Her completely. I know She knows what She is up to while She is calling these circles together. Sometimes they last and sometimes they don't. Some need to dissolve when they have done the job.

CEREMONIAL CIRCLE: You are talking about an organic evolution.

Anthea: Yes. For some reason, the circle form seems to allow that because it is not obvious who is in charge, because there is no "in charge" place.

When you look across the circle you look across the center and the center is where the information comes from. It spirals out and around.

We experience having more authority when we sit in a circle. When we sit looking at someone in front there is an automatic assumption that that person has some authority and we don't have as much. If you raise the person up a couple of steps, there is another biological truth, up is more important. The mind registers that we are referring or deferring to an authority that knows what we don't know.

When we are in a circle, especially if we sit on the ground, people immediately become more related, feel closer to one another. That is their first experience, and secondly they start to go inward to their own authority. There is no place around the circle that can be identified as the place of authority. Then, if we place objects in the center of the circle, each person can relate to them in a very personal way. A lot goes on with that simple physical adjustment.

I think it also makes a safe space. It creates a womb so that everything that is put out from the individual goes into the sacred space in the middle and is held within. It creates a container for everything, whereas, when you are sitting in lines and you put some of yourself out, it is received by the authority figure in the group, rather than the space.

I always hated to be in school because of that authority up there. In a circle I never have the feeling that I'm there to find out from somebody who knows. Everyone in the circle has things to tell me that are new and exciting. The entire experience is inner, more of an exploration of each other with each other. The "Yes, me too!" kind of thing.

It is possible in a circle for everyone to have equal rights toward the center. I don't think there is any other shape that allows that. We can never not be equal in a circle in terms of our access to the center. If there is a performance in the center, or a jewel in the center, or a fire in the center, or a problem in the center, we are all equally near or equally far away. Nobody has the upper hand in that sense.

There is a tension across a circle toward whoever is opposite you. If that is someone you don't like, you have to go across the center, the heart, to meet them. You go from the heart, and they come to you from the heart. If you constantly cross that heart, the center where there is nothing and everything, in order to go anywhere, it will work.

CEREMONIAL CIRCLE: The circle is a very ancient form. Why do you think it is being rediscovered now?

Anthea: Because it is needed and we will all die if it isn't. It is that simple. It's what makes everything else happen. Free will is the ability to not be in circle. It is the ability, the capacity, the choice to screw everything up if we want to. But the natural flow, if you release your "making it happen" mind, is a circle. It is the natural shape.

In my vision the Goddess is material, therefore She is organic and consists of us and we consist of Her. If She is organic and material She is likely to be similar in her larger form to how we are in our smaller form, so I assume that She is composed of cells. My vision is that each circle is a cell in the body of the Goddess of Wisdom. Right now wisdom is beginning to appear on the Earth. We have had knowledge but not much wisdom. Everywhere that a circle forms, a cell of wisdom is in the process of being networked with other cells of wisdom and all these cells are slowly communicating with each other. I have a definite concept of the body of the Goddess of Wisdom being exactly the same as a baby in the womb. The Goddess is DNA and that DNA is in the process of causing certain organs to be built one after another, different limbs being formed.

It has to do with radical authenticity, relationship. It is as if the mind-body split in the individual is reflected in the planet. We have got a network of mind-stuff around the planet that is not in any way interrelated with the biological reality. The things we say to each other, the things we communicate, whether they be objects or words or whatever, are basically unreal, not authentic.

Slowly these authentically relating cells are forming and one by one they are beginning to find one another and starting to join up. If we are lucky, by the grace of the Goddess, authenticity will simply overtake inauthenticity and the structure of deceit will fall apart.

CEREMONIAL CIRCLE: I am hearing that with every authentic act we make, we are creating the body of the Goddess. That is a beautiful image.

Anthea: Yes. I think that's it. It is the energy of relationship and love. When we change to that mode, suddenly fear is gone, hostility is gone, grabbing is gone.

Women are always symbiotically related to everything. What we need is a new symbiosis for the whole world and that is communion. Communion is symbiosis with consciousness. It means we know we are all one, we choose to be all one, and within that all one we each have a very individual and specific gift to bring. I am here to be a part of the oneness.

I see these cells as the embryo of the Goddess taking shape, like you and me sitting here doing this, it is happening all over the place. In Russia, England, everywhere there are people sitting down to talk about souls. At some point there will be a crisis and the network of the body of the Goddess will be so well formed that everyone will call ten of their friends and it will turn out that everyone knows everyone else. Everybody who is in this network will hold hands and stand up, and it will be practically the whole planet and the superstructure will just collapse.

CEREMONIAL CIRCLE: That's a wonderful image.

Anthea: We will all just stand up and the superstructure will fall apart because it is built on us. When we stand up and hold hands it will come off the ground and collapse. That is what is happening, and it will work because it will never be organized. There will be nothing to fight. There will never be a center, or a leader, or anything except some cells here and there, until the body stands up, and it will be the body of the Goddess.

CEREMONIAL CIRCLE: How important is the individual in all this?

Anthea: I see that the base component is individuation, that everybody know themselves as being whole. When you know that you are whole you want to find other people and be whole together with them. It is not very meaningful to be whole all by yourself, so then you want to be in a circle of people who are whole. The criterion is still radical authenticity. If you don't dialogue radically or authentically with anyone, outside or inside, you don't get anywhere.

CEREMONIAL CIRCLE: Why do you say "radical" authenticity?

Anthea: It doesn't brook any messing around. There is no "pretty authentic." It is all radical, down to the roots. It is another way of saying the truth. It is all the way down to the bottom, to the worst, most horrifying, terrifying, dreadful things that you might have to face.

If you want the benefits of synchronicity, serendipity, and grace, which I do because I want miracles, you have to let go. You have to just say what is, do what is, and be what is, and that way you are subject to miracles all the time.

When you are where you need to be, so is everything else. All you need to do is reach out and it is there. That is what I experience. We think when we are inauthentic that we are making things easier, but we are really only complicating everything. That capacity to grit your teeth and tell the truth is essential.

CEREMONIAL CIRCLE: I see why you say it is radical. Really in a cultural context being truthful and authentic is a very radical act. Certainly it is not what we are taught, is it?

Anthea: No, it isn't, and of course it causes the collapse of everything. That is why I say that if we were all radically authentic and stood up and held hands, it would cause the collapse of the structure. Once you start being authentic it blows the whole system. Nothing can stand up any more once you start pulling the threads out.

You get down to questions of love in a circle situation. Love is not about loving everybody. Love is about being radically authentic with everybody. You begin to see in the circle format how you must always live with half a world that isn't you, that you don't understand, that seems very foreign to you, that seems even threatening to you. Then love becomes something quite different, and in a circle you can see that. When you are in a circle it is a complete shape and half of it is opposite to you by its very nature. Whatever it is, it is just opposite to you. It becomes very clear.

I see that everyone in every circle is just me. There is the honest man, and there is the bore, and there is the housewife, and there is the clown, and there is the kid. They are all me. It depends on my consciousness whether that circle becomes real to me. There is a center and an edge of my existence, there is a circle to which I belong. If I am channeling through that center, that radical authenticity, using all the messages that are coming from my circles, I'll get the message and I'll hand it on. It's that simple, because the channels will be clear.

I think that is essentially what the mandala is all about. When you become conscious enough of all the dreams and images and all the things you do, it suddenly shifts itself and becomes what is always was, the invisible circle. The circle with the sacred center.

If you visualize everything as a circle, and yourself always in a circle, there is always a point of reference at the center. The point of reference is always the heart and the radically authentic "I." Somehow with that center, ethics, or whatever it is that you live by, become possible. You stand somewhere. Without that, the sense of the world is disorder, no edges, no point of reference. There is nothing to be responsible to, or responsible for.

CEREMONIAL CIRCLE: That's a fearful position.

Anthea: Yes. You don't know where you are going, or why, where the edge is, who's got it or who's in charge of it. It's as if there is no responsibility—no ability to respond. It is all too big and too amorphous.

It doesn't really matter how large the circle is that you imagine. The circle can be just you and a few friends. If you are always in the circle and the center is not identified with any of you, there is always the awareness of its heart. There is a way to be that gives you a point of reference. I think that is the most important thing about a circle.

VICKI NOBLE

I met with Vicki on a sunny day in a park in Berkeley. She was there with her son who was one year old at the time. Vicki is small and vivacious.

She spoke with great enthusiasm while at the same time amusing her child.

I met her initially at a workshop that she led on the Motherpeace Tarot deck that she had co-created with Karen Vogel. She is a good teacher, full of information about the Goddess and prepatriarchal times. She has a thorough knowledge of symbols and archetypes and her class was rich with feminine imagery.

She has a strong vision of woman power returning. She has written several books on the Tarot and a book about woman power, *Shakti Woman*. She organizes large ceremonial circles in northern California, is deeply involved in the feminist spirituality movement, and has a school for the study of shamanism, emphasizing the study of the Goddess. She is the publisher of *Snake Power*, a journal of contemporary female shamanism.

Circle Is the Wheel of Life

CEREMONIAL CIRCLE: Your Motherpeace cards are circular in shape and contain many images of women in circle. Why is that?

Vicki: It is the feminine form, and it has to do with there being no beginning and no end. I think it represents the whole cycle of consciousness that belongs to the Goddess. All ancient religion of the Goddess centers in some way around the concept of return and return and return. Always we come back to something, or what's out there comes around, and yet each time it's different when it returns. The Goddess religion recognizes the year and the day. Everything happens in a year and a day rather than it just being a year so there is a spiral.

We are always returning but we are never in the same place. I think that is real important because people get hung up on not wanting to repeat anything. Often in response to the idea of the circle, that will be the resistance, so I always work with the idea of the spiral in the circle, so there is movement. There is growth but it is not a linear evolutionary view because I think that is totally patriarchal. It has only been around for five thousand years and before that people were not thinking in terms of having been somewhere and going somewhere. The evolutionary model always puts that in terms of what is behind us is bad and we have gotten out of it, and what is ahead of us is good and we are better than we used to be, and all that seems really damaging.

CEREMONIAL CIRCLE: It makes for a kind of restlessness even, doesn't it?

Vicki: Yes, it does, and a terrible devaluing of the ancestors, which in all native religion is the center of worship. To remember the sacred ancestors and to understand our lineage and to be in contact with those who have gone before. The Goddess religion is so much about that. In the Motherpeace deck the circle is the Zodiacal wheel of life. It is the calendar and the sacred wheel of wholeness.

CEREMONIAL CIRCLE: I'd like you to talk about the historical perspective of people gathering in circles and how that relates to what is happening now.

Vicki: A lot of the work that I have been doing lately is focused on the Sumerian Goddess Inanna, the first Goddess that we know about from historical times. She represents the whole idea of going to the underworld. Very shamanistic kind of imagery. Going to the underworld, meeting your dark side there, coming back up into the light after you have done the work of dying and being reborn. That is a personal circling that was deeply recognized in the old religion in the ancient times before patriarchy. All those structures from that period of time, from before five thousand years ago, all the dwellings that people lived in and the temples that they built, and even the cities, were round or sometimes were in the crescent moon shape. All the places where people lived in the early times were round and I think it was a recognition of the roundness of life. The early writing and the early alphabets were sacred to the priestess and were carried on round clay disks and whatever was written was written in a spiral form.

Stonehenge is an obvious example of all the stones being set in a circle. It is a big power place where people gathered and worshiped together. It was clearly linked to the lunar cycles in a very complex way and to the making of a calendar. The sacred calendar is always round. It shows the holidays, the solstices and the equinoxes, and the four cross-quarter days in between. This is always shown in the round and places like Stonehenge were actually physical calendars. They were set up so that the sun, moon, and planets played on them. The ancients knew so much more than we do about how things move in the heavens and what that movement means to us here.

All of that is really deeply related to the fact that people came together in circles, to recognize that and to witness it, and to raise energy. It has apparently always been known that if you gather together in a circle and run energy, the energy gets really big, and then you can use it. It seems they were using power in ancient times for really amazing things that are hard to conceive of, such as moving big rocks and changing structures and doing regenerative healing. They were doing everything in groups and circles.

When you do group work and you put a person who is sick in the center of a circle and do a healing on them it is really different than if you, as a healer, work on them individually. The circle is so powerful and its focus so great that it intensifies it exponentially. As a healer you can feel that in the circle. There is a really big difference.

Whatever we do in a circle is always more powerful than what we do alone. It always raises the energy to the heart level. I think it is a magical reality. You hold hands and you start meditating together. Even when I've had people just breathe together and they are not praying, it still moves the energy to the heart level. It is a miracle.

CEREMONIAL CIRCLE: You implied that in the healing circle the group becomes one. Do you think that is typical of circles?

Vicki: Yes, I think that is the whole thing that happens. It must be connected to the heart chakra automatically. The heart chakra could be represented by a circle. It is about union, oneness, a circle of people who become one entity. If you do it with intention it ups the ante again and makes it even more powerful than when you use it without having a sense of its power.

Lately I've been wanting to get back to more of the ancient unstructured circling, where the community gathers in a circle for the purpose of experiencing the energies in an ecstatic way, which in itself is healing. I think we could direct that into different places. I really believe that when we make the circle in the beginning that is what we come there to do and whatever we do inside the circle is not too relevant. It's nice, you could do almost anything, any kind of new age study or healing is just fine, you could even just share with each other, and I think it would be on a higher level. It is making the circle that is actually what I feel we are doing there.

I feel that we are actually gaining the focus, the ability to hold the circle. There is such a need to come into contact together and we need to learn how.

CEREMONIAL CIRCLE: And we learn to do it by doing it?

Vicki: Exactly, every time we do a circle of any kind I feel that something is happening. The changes are finally happening and it has been happening on the etheric level for some time. That is why it is so nourishing to come together in circles. There is a recognition of that and we all move to that level together and then we are in harmony about what is really happening. Otherwise we are going around in our personal lives trying to get our trips together.

CEREMONIAL CIRCLE: Would you say the circle is an immanent form?

Vicki: Yes. It's about the earth. It's about really being here in our lives without escaping, about taking responsibility for what is happening in the moment.

CEREMONIAL CIRCLE: Why are circles coming back right now?

Vicki: I think it has to do with the feminine, and I think it has to do with the fact that we have gone as far as we could go with the linear. If we go any further with it we will destroy ourselves. So in a certain metaphorical sense we are stretched out to the maximum and we need to circle back. The feminine is manifesting again on this planet, the feminine ray, the seventh ray. The seventh ray has to do with ceremony and magic, ritual.

Some old energy that we see in the Stonehenge monument is coming back and becoming available again on our planet and it is the energy of the circle. The return of the circle is so embracing. Nothing else could restore our unity, it has been so broken. I always think of the Goddess as the Mother with her arms around us. There is some special way that we can be held inside of a sacred circle. Inside of a sacred circle anything can happen and we are protected. It is magical for building power and it is a safe space for defending ourselves, for keeping out negative energies and building the positive. It is a magical form more than anything else, and it wasn't utilized for such a long time.

CEREMONIAL CIRCLE: Certainly there is no room for hierarchy in circle.

Vicki: It is not a pyramid, has not got edges. Everyone is equal. I think the egalitarianism of the ancient world is reflected in that. I think the forces that are working on us now want us to get over feeling special and different and so unique and so superior. They want us to feel our connection to everybody else and to feel that we are just like all people. The women's movement is so good at saying that. Mothers are mothers everywhere and they care about their children and they want life to go on. And so Womanness, expressed as peacemaker and peacekeeper, is sort of a universal symbol, and we can join together and experience that unification.

CEREMONIAL CIRCLE: What would you say to people who want to start and meet in circles but are just beginning to consider the idea?

Vicki: I would say just do it, just do it. Come together and see what happens because it is always magical. Even two people, when they get together and hold hands, experience their energy beginning to move in a new way. It is Tantric. You can always expect that something will happen, that it will be healing, sometimes it will be exciting, and at least it will be balancing. Something always takes place, a shift. Some kind of a smoothing of the edges in our energy bodies, and a coming together. It is really such a miraculous experience to hold hands with other people and feel the differences dissolve and feel the commonness. I would say that people should just do that. I often feel that form gets in our way and people get really locked in to "doing it right."

CEREMONIAL CIRCLE: So we should just trust the form and the energy of the circle to direct us.

Vicki: Yes, because it will do us then, we don't have to do it. We can actually be worked on. In a sense, much that is happening right now is a willingness to be acted on by the forces.

CEREMONIAL CIRCLE: That is a big leap in consciousness.

Vicki: It is a *big* leap. It is an understanding that there are helping forces and they are bigger than we are and we can actually use the circle to call them in. They are attracted to it. Whenever there is a circle it's like a magnet for the healing energies.

When you get in a circle with people and you start letting the energy flow there is a certain amount of oracular opening that takes place. If people could trust that they might begin to actually access information and direct their own evolution in circles.

CEREMONIAL CIRCLE: So, all of this should be very threatening to the status quo!

Vicki: Yes! Very! I am envisioning huge circles now. Really large circles of people imagining world peace. Basically we would just breathe together and focus our energy toward making the leap. A way of leaping out of our old mind-sets about what is reality and into something new. It is hovering, it is really there. Something is close and it is going to move us to another level. I have been feeling a kind of a pull.

CEREMONIAL CIRCLE: It seems to me in my own life that the longing for community is very strong. A community where all the things that we have learned can be used in a vital way.

Vicki: I think that it hasn't really manifested other than in a small way because as a culture, a society, we haven't actually felt pushed to the point where we must, and when we have to we will. We need to be really deep with each other. One thing that can take away the fear of that is to be in circles, in groups, because it moves the energy to the heart level and then it is not so frightening. I am not speaking so much of the one-on-one personal intimate connection which we are learning, but a more impersonal connecting and it's lovely, you know. It is very healing, and there is an acceptance there. I think it provides an opportunity for us to learn to be transparent and really be accepted and loved for who we are in our uniqueness. I think the circle makes that possible.

At first there is a fear, but we have such an unconscious longing to be close and not be so isolated that it breaks through, and it doesn't take long. Only a minute or two and all of a sudden it is as if everybody is humming together, the energy just relaxes and immediately raises. There is an incredible opening and it helps us to move to the group level without all that fear.

You can't talk about it, you just have to experience it. As we do that more and more in groups it will be easier to actually become intimate with each other, and not be so terrified on that level. Then people will be able to hold relationships and hold the focus. I am working with larger groups of people, in circles, and getting them to sing. When we sing in a circle of people and put our energies together in that rhythmic kind of a way, you can feel the chakras opening and the energies moving to a higher level.

ELIZABETH COGBURN

Elizabeth and her husband, Robert, arrived quite unexpectedly at my house late on a cold and rainy February night. They had been camping on the beach and their tent had collapsed on them. I had known them for many years and have participated in Elizabeth's dance ceremonials. Their arrival was dramatic and exciting, just as all things seem to be with Elizabeth. She is a remarkable woman, full of energy and fire and great enthusiasm for life. They spent several days with us, filling my tiny house with a great deal of fun and laughter, and a lot of learning for me, as well. She is a very wise woman and can always be counted on to speak directly and honestly. We began our interview on a late afternoon in Joshua's large living room by doing some drumming and singing together. Elizabeth never once sat down while we were taping her words. Instead she danced the interview. She is a beautiful woman in her middle fifties, full of vitality and energy. She is amazingly articulate and so sure of her words that we gave up any pretense of directing the course of the interview. Instead we listened appreciatively, allowing her to follow her own flowing, dancing current.

Elizabeth is a Western Cabalist who for the past twenty-five years has been working with a growing circle of friends who live all around the country, creating magnificent ceremonial dances that honor the solstices, equinoxes, and the midpoints. These big ceremonials are created as a dramatic alternative to the destructive dramas of our civilization.

Dancing on the Edge

CEREMONIAL CIRCLE: Elizabeth, I'd like to ask you some questions about creating circle and building community.

Elizabeth: Our New Song Community did not set out to make a circle. We set out as a group of individuals. A great many of the people who came were loners. We came out of the woods and sagebrush, into a clearing, and we just wanted to sing and dance and drum our hearts out. We weren't thinking about community and we weren't thinking about making circles. We just found that we had to if we were going to do what we wanted to do.

We grew into a circle of people searching for something we needed. I believe this is the rule of the circle, it is a response to something you need. Real living ritual is rooted in human need, which means there is presence to it. It means you are there with your full being. So, in the early days we came together and we knew it was taking us somewhere.

We instinctively knew we wanted to put up a pole, and we wanted to do it at the biggest sun time of the year. We went out into the desert at the summer solstice. We wanted *bare* earth and *big* sky and *blazing* sun. We wanted to drum. We didn't want any drugs, we didn't need them. Gradually more and more people came and they were people with staying power. That became the Sun Dance.

We went to Native American lodge ceremonies and learned a lot about ceremonial process. We'd study how they were with their energy. How do you mix eating and dancing a long time? We'd look at all those people at the corn dances and how they'd keep their concentration strong and still exist in transpersonal space. You can go to a corn dance and see a whole tribe in the transpersonal realm. We learned a lot, but we were never imitating anybody else. We have always been consciously dedicated to finding and trusting our own forms.

Our ground was in those generic elements that all humanity has always done, beginning with making circles. Apes make circles, even dance in them. *It's in the DNA.*

CEREMONIAL CIRCLE: A problem with communities is getting staying power, so there must have been some alchemy that was happening to inspire that.

Elizabeth: Sure, you had to be getting something that was so good you would set aside a period of time every year to go back and do it, just because it was the best show going.

So the circle formed as a resultant pattern, from the pulse of shared need and longing. Our drummer would always say to me that the melody was the resultant pattern of the pulse. If you can get your one-one-one beat going, all the songs of the universe are contained there. He was right. The drum is definitely the foundation. When you have a strong pulse all sentient beings in a field will be entrained in the strongest rhythm present. We would hold the pulse of the drum for hours. We would start when the full moon came up over Taos Mountain and end when the sun came. The drumming made the ground.

We discovered images from Mircea Eliade's writings. People would come back and say, "Those old shamans would do their drumming and lay out a Rainbow Path that everybody danced on." And we'd say, "Yeah, that's what it feels like." So we came into a lot of it in reverse, by getting there and doing it and then finding out what it was about.

CEREMONIAL CIRCLE: How did you come into your shamanic intention and power?

Elizabeth: The way my training has worked is you just get out in life and you live, you "take on assignments," you put yourself on the edge. You are your own disciplinarian. You withdraw the projection of the outer authority and you risk to take authorship for yourself. You can tell by the way it feels which experiences are initiations, and you give yourself to them fully, putting your life on the line. You see what is coming and how fast you can transform it. That's part of how you come into your power. My assignments have been in the service of a Community of Spirit, as a midwife of soul in ceremonial theater.

The Long Dances emerged from the Sun Dance automatically. It was meaning so much to us we decided to have more dances so we danced on the equinoxes and solstices and the cross-quarter days. What we've done, in essence, is create context. We realized we needed community. The best times and the best folks and the richest tapestry of daily life were happening to us in relation to one another, some real alchemy.

We are, and always have been, a Community of Spirit, gathered at appointed times from all over the country to create a ceremonial theater of soul-making to inquire into and learn the wisdom teachings which comprise the guiding pattern/story/myth we choose to live by. We enact and practice embodying aspects of our individual stories, and our shared story, in transformational ritual dance/drama.

What bonds and binds us together is our longing to share the adventure of our soul's journey toward wholeness with others of like intent and intensity. Although we originally gathered to drum, sing, and dance, we very quickly became aware that this was not enough. We felt a need to clarify what and whom we were dancing for and about. A desire to dedicate and direct the energy of the dance into specific personal and cultural changes. Thus the ritual of the Talking Staff Circles came into being, in which we seek to witness one another in the clarification of our intentions to change actions, in our lives and our home/world communities, between the dances.

I believe that a major aspect of the alchemy we experience in our work is the continuity of our shared cycling through phases of action in the dance and in the world. Then, through reflection upon the consequences and meanings of our actions, and the witnessing of one another over the years, we bloom like flowers into ever more conscious, creative, and satisfying living.

Because our focus is on the inner life, the transformations of consciousness toward greater integration and inner experience of a unitive state, it has been a strength for our community to have loose physical boundaries. We gather in the ceremonials as a time and place to step back from our daily lives to reflect, regroup our energies and outlooks, practice new ways of being, that we might return to our homes with new insights, perspectives, attitudes, and commitments, intending to more effectively "walk what we are talking."

As Sun Bear says, "if your philosophy does not grow corn I don't want to hear about it." We all seek to "grow better corn" in all of our relationships at home and at work. Our ability to sustain this effort at home is greatly enhanced by knowing that the next ceremonial gathering is on the calendar.

CEREMONIAL CIRCLE: You grounded your spiritual into the political, into the earth.

Elizabeth: A lot of people in the New Age community are beginning to take seriously that there is no division between spirituality and politics. In the essence of the spiritual, and in what politics are really about, Gandhi was absolutely right when he said that people who think there is a separation between spirituality and politics don't understand what spirituality is. I would say they don't understand what politics is either. When you combine them your life becomes a work of art, your community becomes a work of art.

CEREMONIAL CIRCLE: I'm so glad to hear you say that.

Elizabeth: We're working on it from two angles. We're totally in the position that your spiritual development is measured and expressed by how you are living this life and caring for this planet, in and through the physical. That is our teaching. Do not waste your physical body; *you are the earth*. It is not a question of you and nature. You are an absolute functioning organ of the life of this planet Earth, and as you conduct yourself, so will the earth be.

Another thing our teachings say is that all human beings will misuse all powers until they learn how to use them rightly. That's why we're here, to learn how to use them rightly. It does not just happen. It has to be recognized and sought after and courted and cultivated. What is power? What are the various powers and how do we know when we are using them right?

CEREMONIAL CIRCLE: It seems to me that you are using the circle and the community as a vehicle for learning about this use of power.

Elizabeth: That's true. We came eventually to a *very* important piece of our evolution, to where we had taken just doing dances as far as it could go. We knew the energy had to change. At this point, in the sixties, I think a lot of people hit hard drugs because they didn't know how to take the next creative, life-making step. They knew you had to go further, and didn't know how to do it. You've *got* to have the wilderness of the soul. Somehow, by grace we were shown something else. We had been going slowly, slowly, like it takes a good tree to grow, you know. Gradually we began to put our cabala studies together with our dances.

I'm after the evolution of human consciousness, the creation of a humane sustainable culture, and the cultivation of sacred ecstasy. It's a common human way to express ourselves violently when we do not have a right path. In a down-home, country way, I'd say, "We're doing what we're doing to bring abundance and well-being to all beings. It's for happiness." Cabala says it's for pleasure; the tendency of consciousness is toward pleasure. And you say, "Oh, yeah, but what kind of pleasure?" And the cabala says to you, "Delight." "Well, what kind of delight?" "Well, rapture." "Well, what kind of rapture?" "Well, *ecstasy!*" "Well, what kind of ecstasy?" "Well union with the *one*. What else is there?" And so saying "to bring happiness to the people" is shorthand.

I think that the community has to always be rooted in the real needs of the people, needs of the deep souls as well as the body, in harmony with all life, under the guidance of wisdom teachings.

So, we had a circle. We were even given a gold ring by the Sun Dance Pole. It was lost in the dirt and months later it was returned to us right under the Pole. And the Pole said, "This is the ring that has been returned and you are to understand that you are the ring that has been returned. You have had to go out and do individually in order to become conscious, and now is the time to form the ring of consciousness."

What does it *mean* to be returning as conscious beings to the circle, committing to make a circle? We say that the circle is unconditional love. There's plenty of times when I'm just not too sure in the daily grit that I love you, and it's not unconditional at all. You know, I have to sort it out. Do I still love you? Do I still love you even though I'd like to wring your neck? I'd like to crack your head. I'd like you out of my picture. All the stuff that just naturally comes up as part of the evolution of the human condition.

It began to seem that if we had the form, we could always come back and make a circle again, and say "Yeah, but in the big picture of course I still love you. I'm in here for the duration and as long as we want to work on our stuff together, and get more real, I'm up for it. I'll be here." *That* was important.

My husband and I knew from the beginning that whether the ceremony happened or not depended on whether we said to the sun, or the gods, or the center, or whatever we called it, "Whether anybody else is there or not, I will be there." We never got hooked into thinking "people have got to come." Always decide that you yourself are going to do it no matter what, and if anybody else wants to come, fine.

That has to do with somebody holding the power in the center. It has been my understanding that my assignment at this time on the planet is to be here as one who *holds* power in the dance, as a demonstration, as a catalyst. A lot of my training has been in how to do this, really to be a servant to the center pole, which is the tree of life. I am simply a servant, and, in particular, I call Sun Dances. That puts me right in the middle of the tree. That puts me in the sphere as a daughter, an agent of beauty, or however you would put it.

Anywhere you go you can recreate sacred space, the temple. People with the biggest brute force have always gone in and demolished the temples of the conquered in order to dis-ensoul and dis-spirit them. Wherever we are is *it*, is the Tree of Life. Our temple of wisdom and truth is inside us and no matter how many buildings are destroyed the real temple lives on within us, whether we are in physical bodies or not. You can dance in any meadow, any grove, they're all over the world. They become enlivened and empowered by our relationship with them.

CEREMONIAL CIRCLE: How essential has it been for the process to have that place that you return to over and over again, your ground?

Elizabeth: In our years of evolution I can identify different phases. In the early days we had regular meeting places in Taos, one in the ceremonial room of our home and one on a powerful piece of public land at the rim of the Rio Grande. Then there was a ten-year period when I lived on the road, as a "circuit rider." During this period I wove trails back and forth across America and Canada creating ritual dances at the invitation of local groups. We found that almost any room can be turned into a "temple" or ceremonial theater, and that there are powerful places on the earth in all regions. It is our own creative imaginations and heartful intention that can always create sacred place/space. That it is our shared longing, intention, willingness to engage in the high play of the ceremonial theater, and ulti-mately our common humanness that bonds each circle into a community.

Out of this circuit riding, several ongoing local ritual drumming and dancing communities were generated and developed in accordance with their own needs, visions, and circumstances. Members of these come back to the New Song Ceremonials for the special stimulation and inspiration they find with us.

We began to do our Sun Dance in a wonderful little meadow in the Jemez Mountains in New Mexico. In this place we could leave the dance pole up from year to year. This place, as much as we loved it, required considerable effort to get people and gear into over miles of cliff-hanging dirt roads and muddy trails. Keeping the dance and camp together during torrential rains was a wonderful teaching, but came in time to seem like distractions and unnecessary burdens.

When a drought made it impossible for us to return to the meadow it was with considerable relief and delight that we moved the Sun Dance back to our retreat house in New Mexico. Now we hold all our yearly cycle of ceremonials here.

We are being given a whole new set of teachings that come from staying put and attending the growth and development of this one place and ourselves in relation to this dimension of continuity. Planting trees, mudding the adobe house walls, treasuring every drop of water, recycling, dancing on the ground in the winter snow and summer heat, feeling our souls and lives growing in natural, organic rhythm along with all the other beings around us. With this shift we deepen more and more into the intimacy of our community of Spirit in which our intention is not to be "perfect," or "nice," but to be *real*, in finding harmony, strength, and beauty in our diversity.

We have a line dance that we do at which we chant: "Road/Home, Road/Home, Road/Home," to honor the part of ourselves that has to have that grounded, rooted place and the other side that's *gotta* fly.

CHOQOSH AUH-HO-OH

Choqosh Auh-ho-oh is a warrior woman of Chumash Indian ancestry. She is a very articulate teacher, drawing on her own roots, Hopi and Apache training, as well as Zen Buddhism, Tantra, and the Tao. I first met her in June of 1986. My friend Jana and I were traveling home from a visit to the Southwest and we had made arrangements to stop by Choqosh's house in Pacific Grove, California, to deliver a drum that she had ordered from a mutual friend. She lives in a very nice and modest house hidden away on a quiet street with her daughter, Spring.

Choqosh has a powerful presence. She is tall and full-bodied with beautiful black eyes, long black hair, and a very large aura. She welcomed us as if we were her returning sisters who had been separated by great time and space but who had been loved and longed for daily. We were fed and entertained and then went to the ocean where we co-created a circle ceremony.

Our spontaneous circle was joined by a very curious and lively young seal who seemed to especially respond to one particular song that we sang. The inclusion into our circle of this beautiful being was a very great and special blessing. We felt the active presence of the seal to be an affirmation of the power that can be generated through the circle. It was a clear sign that consciousness is much less limited than we imagine.

Choqosh was delighted that this circle, convened in one of her power spots, had welcomed a visitor from the sea who had appreciated and joined us in our song. The experience created a very special bond between us. It was powerful to see our circle grow in this way.

Coming 'Round Full Circle

CEREMONIAL CIRCLE: Would you share with us some of your feelings about the circle process?

Choqosh: I have a lot of feelings about the circle, a love affair with the circle. I'll tell you a few things that native people have to say about the circle. It is sacred, because all things in life are a circle. Everything comes in a circle. Those parts of our bodies which open to receive the sacredness of life and the gifts of the Creator are circles. Our lives begin from babyhood, then as children, as adults, as elders, and returning to being children again we are all a circle.

The seasons are a circle. When people come together in council and enjoy together they are in a circle. The circle is sacred because it honors all people as one. There is no beginning, there's no end. There is no one that's higher, no one that's lower. No one is separate in a circle. As you can see, it is a most blessed, blessed form.

The Chumash people and the Hopi people talk about the circle. They say that once the truth was whole and known by every being, all the truth, the language of the animals and the stones and the water and the air. We were all family and there was no separation.

They say that an imbalance came, and when that happened the circle was broken and the whole of the truth was divided, and once the whole was divided the parts needed names. They were sent with the names of their clans and each was responsible for their portion of the truth. They were to go out and re-find this truth and someday return and remember who they were and their connection with one another and their responsibility. They were to remember that they were caretakers of the truth.

But they forgot after a period of time and began to think that they had the only truth and became protectors instead of caretakers. Their truth and their spirituality became religions that divided them from, and created a lack of respect for, other people. Masala, the messenger of the Hopi people, told them that there would again come a great imbalance to the Earth, and once again we would experience an eleventh hour and would have the choice before us to live out of balance and destroy, or to come back within the balance of life.

This is happening in our time, where the ability to communicate in circles comes from the Earth, and we are able to receive the knowledge, wisdom, and beauty of that portion of the truth that was given the people of the North, the people of the East, and the people of the South, and now at the last moment there is the one missing piece. That is the knowledge and the truth that comes from the people of the West and that is the symbol of living in balance. Of life here on Earth being a heaven, a paradise, where we are created, taken care of and nurtured in the midst of the most incredible gifts of the Creator.

This is paradise here, and it is sacred. In living our lives in a sacred manner and knowing in our relationship to all things that we are no greater and no less. This completes the full circle. Completes all the information and the balance of knowledge and wisdom that we require to live in peace and harmony again.

Now it is coming around full circle after going so far away from the Earth and the simplicity of things. It's the celebration of songs without dogma, churches without walls, and just the joy of the divine, this great life-force Spirit and this incredible gratitude. It doesn't divide us. It includes everyone. It is a full circle.

CEREMONIAL CIRCLE: People are sitting in circles now more and more. Do you think that perhaps it is synchronous with the Sacred Hoop being returned to wholeness?

Choqosh: People are beginning to trust their intuition. People are beginning to trust their sensitivity and the spirit within them, and they are listening. In listening now they are moved intuitively to do things which are most appropriate. It is happening everywhere in the world simultaneously. It is time for the mending of the Sacred Hoop, for returning full circle and recognizing our part in that.

I have noticed that even in educational and medical institutions they are starting to talk about a holistic way, the full circle. I know when I have tried to teach my classes within the confinements of a classroom, where there are chairs sitting behind one another in rows, and I'm in the front and they are out there, and we are all looking at one another's backs, the message just doesn't come through.

When we break away from linear lines and rows and standing one behind another, and move into a circle where we can see each other, where the information and the Spirit teachings come through, we make of ourselves a crucible, like the alchemist's bowl. All the chemistry of our beings, from our different countries, our ancestors, our experiences, who we are, the chemistry of our faces and the different looks, creates in the circle the Holy Grail. We are that which has been sought. We are that.

The Holy Grail, as I understand, was made out of silver or gold or diamonds, things that are tempered by great pressure and by fire. I think that the journey of our lives in search of the Holy Grail, and all we go through in the fire of life, tempers us. It brings out the gleam, the preciousness, the resilience, as it does in steel.

I think that we need to reacquaint ourselves and rethink our thoughts concerning dark nights of the soul. I think we put a negative aspect to them because they are painful and they make us fearful. We go into questioning every aspect of our being. But think what a healthy exercise that is: we clean the basket, we burn away the chaff. People forget, maybe it takes surviving for a while through our thirties and into our forties. You begin to see the pattern that after the darkest night of the soul, when you feel so unworthy you even question going on, that something extraordinary comes. Dark nights of the soul don't end whimpering. You come to a turn in the road and the sun is there! You have survived one more time.

CEREMONIAL CIRCLE: Another circle.

Choqosh: Another circle! But they don't teach us that because we broke the circle with our elders, because we keep them apart from us. We don't sit at their feet and listen to their wisdom. They are able to teach simply the patterns of one's life, seeing in great perspective from having done many circles over and over again. Because our teachers are cut off from elders, and the circle is broken, the spiraling of information gleaned from ancestor to ancestor to ancestor has been lost.

We are really very stupid, because we are having to learn everything over again brand-new. We didn't know how to raise children or live with a spouse or deal with the dark nights of the soul. Nobody told us that everybody went through it, and that it is a gift. It means that you are at work, the process is on.

CEREMONIAL CIRCLE: In the same vein we are having to learn again something as simple as sitting in circles. Learn about that form and containing the energy that is in that form. Why do you think that is returning?

Choqosh: Because it's time. Because this is the eleventh hour. Because we have been doing what we have been doing and watching things happen. Calling black white, and calling medical treatments healing, and educational institutions teaching—and none of them are. We have everything backwards and everything upside down. So many religions negate life and refuse to celebrate the gifts of the Creator. The most beautiful things of all are things they say you must deny if you are truly religious. How can you deny a gift of God without it being pure heresy? That is sin! That is wastefulness.

I feel it is coming back now because this is the eleventh hour that the Hopis talk about. We have certainly gone out of balance, broken the circles, and everything that we create are things that destroy, things that poison. Some people say that a while back this Earth was seeded, like a garden, with souls, and that the coming of seasons has happened and now it is time for harvest. The time of ripening is here.

Other people say that at the point of the eleventh hour, when we have taken confusion and doubt, violence and greed, all imbalance as far as it can go on this paradise, that we will come to a critical mass of consciousness. Some people call it the "hundredth monkey." Physicists and biologists are now beginning to join with Rupert Sheldrake in talking about morphic resonance. I think that we are a majority and it is getting faster and more complete. More people are shedding the old laws, the artificiality that has been created in this life. Every one of us that wakes up emanates this energy and helps to open it in those around us.

I believe it is going so fast that every day it almost doubles in intensity and the speed in which people are being touched. Much like when there is conception and a single cell and it goes into two and then four and then eight, each giving birth and duplicating itself. I think we have been in a place of great darkness. It cannot get any darker before we destroy ourselves. The pendulum is swinging back. We are coming full circle. It is a time for the light.

It is perhaps full circle time. We have gone through the winter. It is the time of the owl. It is very interesting how these things begin to happen simultaneously everywhere, whether you are a scientist, a musician, or simply a human being who begins to become sensitive to the animals and to the symbology, the sacred metaphor in everything. All of a sudden, wherever I go, I am meeting owl women.

There are a lot of wolf people around too, which is a beautiful thing. The wolves are like the dolphins of the land: They live in community, there are never orphans, they take care of each other, they mate for life, males and females hunt equally and also take care of the children. All are cared for. These wolf-people are people who sense community. They are the community builders, the bringer-backers of family.

There has been in wolves, as with the dolphin and with the owl, a communication with people for a long time. There are many stories and they are true. The owl, like other birds, signifies a certain aspect of the human being or energies that are in the world. The owl is an extraordinary bird, and no small spirit vibration at all. The owl is sacred for many Californian Indian people, and frankly I think it must have been for all Indian peoples at one time before they forgot and started looking for superstitions and fears, before they thought that the Creator could possibly have created an evil animal.

For the Chumash Indian people the owl is the Medicine Bird. It is the transformer, the one that sees the light in the darkness. When Chumash Indian people are doing a great healing they use owl feathers. Maybe some people have a reason to fear the owl because it represents the death of ego and the death of confusion, of all that is out of balance. Wherever there is disease it brings the end of that and the renewal, or rebirth, or the bringing into light of health and balance and light. It doesn't do it gently. Our transitions, our changes don't come gently.

Overall we keep prodding and we keep learning, and our circles are spirals. But when we really take a quantum leap in our consciousness it is akin to being born. There is the labor and there is the crowning and the *whoosh!* Then there is the disconnection and the cutting free, until we can stand alone, breathing our own breath and circulating our own blood.

Nature is the signature of God. Understanding nature, you begin to see the metaphor, the microcosmic law, the macrocosmic law, that is within us every moment. We don't have to be incredibly wise. We just need to open our eyes and see what we live in. How is nature? How are the cycles? What is the circle? Then there shouldn't be any confusion as to who we are, and how we will survive in harmony, and what happens to us when we get out of that. Look at nature. Look at the signature of God. That is the Bible, those are the Laws. And it doesn't require you to believe. You *look* and see before your eyes.

I spent all of my youth being absolutely suicidal. To me life was a place of injustice and disharmony and people were cruel to each other. I saw the sickness and the disease, and although I was but three years old at the time, I knew when they dropped the bomb on Hiroshima and Nagasaki. I felt it. It reverberated throughout this world. Nothing was ever quite the same. I really didn't want to be here. I used to go to my closet and sit and pray to God, if there was one, to get me out of here. I wanted my body to leave, but I was into having my eyes stick around somehow if I could, to just watch. I didn't want to be a part of it.

One day a woman named Bee who lived on an organic farm in California saw my pain, saw my sorrow. She took me by the hand and led me into the garden. She cleared the cobwebs of my eyes and she showed me the plants, how they breathe, how they would move. When she would pass there would be no wind, but they would turn as though to follow her with their leaves. Through her and her love and communication with them I could begin to hear the song of the plants. To feel their great love and their devotion to life, their incredibly beautiful harmony. The beauty of a kumquat plant was in just being a kumquat. In its fullness it was a glorious kumquat, and it grew and touched the soil, and it took in the air and the water, and it reached to the sky and it gave fruit. It was enough. It was so perfect in what it did and it served so much. It didn't aspire to be anything else. I realized that we are like that. We are what we are. Each of us individually is given at the moment of birth a sacred truth, a strength.

In the old days, when we lived in circles of sacred societies and teaching places, the elders would help us to define that truth, find out who we were, what was our gift. Then in our lives we would re-find that gift, through the dark nights of the soul and the joy and so forth, we would re-find that gift and then give it back to our people.

There was the circle. You received, you re-found it, you were responsible for it and you gave it back. That was all you had to do. A human being, really being human. In that moment you rediscovered your divinity and your strength and your power. And if we are just that, just as we are, we re-find that which we are. Keep it clean, you know. We are given this temple to be housekeepers, caretakers. And then we invite people to the feast!

DOLORES LACHAPELLE

Dolores LaChapelle lives in Silverton, Colorado, at the foot of the Rockies that she loves so much. She is an archivist and synthesizer of consciousness, leads wilderness experiences, teaches T'ai Chi, and is a passionate aficionada of powder skiing. She is the author of three important books in the fields of ceremony and the reclaiming of earth consciousness. *Earth Festival*, published in 1973, was a seminal work in the field. Her recent work, *Sacred Land, Sacred Sex*, is an encompassing and detailed exposition into deep ecology.

We spoke in her home, a small and simple house on a back street in an old silver-mining town, surrounded by huge mountains. Her living room is also her office, filled with desks, books, papers, a testimony to her dedication to her work. She is a slender woman, full of passionate intensity for cultural renewal. She has a deep involvement with her bioregion and the importance of caring for the earth.

Circling with the Seasons

CEREMONIAL CIRCLE: Why is the ceremonial circle returning?

Dolores: Because that's the way everybody did it for as long as we've been human. The basic way of meeting for the Native Americans was in a circle because there was no one chief and that distributed the power around the whole group. They had leaders but they didn't have the same leadership all the time. They had a war-chief, a peace-chief, and if they went down to get salt, they had another chief. They changed leadership continually.

Leadership is important. The circle times are when everybody is giving input, but you can't do everything that way. Day-to-day decisions should be made by someone or it gets too complex. Anyone who has been in a circle prefers the circle because that's the way things work best.

CEREMONIAL CIRCLE: How does sitting in a circle relate to connecting with your place on the earth?

Dolores: Let's go back to the Celtic people. They met in circular rows. The place was open, in between circles of trees. The Greeks also met in groves of trees. Then they cut all the trees down and made wooden poles, then they made marble poles and then they made Greek temples. Greek temples originally were circular. You were in the center looking out between the posts and the goddess was the mountain, as you saw it between the posts. Now we take that Greek architecture to be the posts. See the difference? Originally it was a circle of posts and you looked outside where the different mountains were. That was a way of centering the energy on the particular place you were meeting, because it was a circle and held it in. The circle is the sacred place, the place where no energy is leaked.

CEREMONIAL CIRCLE: The idea of commitment to place seems really important right now.

Dolores: It is. You're absolutely right. I tell people in workshops, in Gary Snyder's words, to go out and find a place you love enough to stay there and fight for it the rest of your life. If you don't love any place that much, there is no point in staying there, you might as well travel. People should travel all over until they find a place that they really care for, then stay there. Develop a real sense of continuity. When we don't stay anywhere we essentially lose the local gods and goddesses because you can't find them if you don't know where they are living.

CEREMONIAL CIRCLE: If you know you're going to leave a place, you often feel you don't have to really care what happens to it. Perhaps if we find a place, stay in it, do circle and ceremony it becomes impossible to exploit it.

Dolores: The original cultures had to pay attention to the land itself because it told them what to do. They didn't destroy it because they had to live there. The original thing was to live in one place and find out what the place wanted from you. Nobody overpopulated until modern times, till Christianity came, because they were smart enough to know that if you lived in this one valley and you had too many kids, you couldn't feed them all.

CEREMONIAL CIRCLE: What is the importance of circling in place as a way to protect the earth?

Dolores: Well, there are several different aspects. Some people are suggesting that everyone adopt a piece of land near them that they want to take care of and then you can pay attention when someone is trying to use it unethically. You know who is going to try to cut the trees or is overgrazing and you can do something about it. If you set it up as the place where you are worshiping, it is your church, like the Taos Indians have Blue Lake. They won that court battle and won the right to worship at Blue Lake after they lost it a hundred years ago.

Let's talk about ethology, which is the study of human and animal behavior. The body wants to worship because the higher primates worship. There was a rain dance ceremony among the chimps that Jane Goodall witnessed and wrote about. Gorillas in another part of Africa used to always come to a particular waterfall and sit there and watch it. That's meditating. It is older than humans, this sense of worship of nature. It is not a hard thing to do. It's innate in the human being.

CEREMONIAL CIRCLE: What kinds of ceremony do you do in your own locality?

Dolores: The thing I do locally is the autumn equinox. I take people up to these particular wild spots and we open with a peak ceremony. We set it up so that the sun on the equinox does its own ritual. We sit up at a hut and chant until the sun sets. Meanwhile, all sorts of things happen.

Once we had an Adams Peak phenomenon. The Adams Peak is sacred to the Jains and the Hindus and many others. When clouds are in a certain area, the peak is projected out over the area. On this equinox the sun was very low and all of a sudden there was a big blue mountain in the middle of my own valley! That was real exciting. There's no mountain in the middle of that valley and here was this huge blue mountain! That was the kind of thing that primitives saw all the time in their place because the light creates those things. It's real exciting when it's your own place that it happens in.

CEREMONIAL CIRCLE: So you gather in a circle and witness the earth and the elements.

Dolores: They do all the work, they show it to you. On the equinox I lead circles and we do chanting. People who come together to chant automatically sit in a circle because they can resonate across and that is just the normal way to do it.

CEREMONIAL CIRCLE: How does one begin the process of going back to who you are and of going back to the earth?

Dolores: Through rituals that are not timed by humans. That's really important. Don't set the time when it's most convenient for you to do it, when nobody is doing any other work or it's after work. Set the time when the moon is full or when the moon is new, the time that nature sets. That's a really important first step because then you are letting nature make the decisions.

CEREMONIAL CIRCLE: That's a real departure from the way things are usually done.

Dolores: Yes, it is. It's a lot more inconvenient. It would be nice if we could do it on a weekend, but making the effort to do it when the moon is full is a first step because you're letting the moon decide when you're going to do the ritual instead of you deciding.

CEREMONIAL CIRCLE: Relinquishing control.

Dolores: And it's really hard. Getting all the brains together so they can bypass the rational hemisphere is very important, that is what ritual is about. Chanting, drumming, all of that is to get you out of the rational hemisphere so that you can really connect. Gregory Bateson, a quite brilliant man, says "The rational hemisphere alone is necessarily pathogenic," that means, necessarily out to kill you, not occasionally or once in a while or by accident, but necessarily, by its nature. What that means on a larger level is that the rational hemisphere was developed by the whole brain as a tool to take things apart and analyze them. It takes things apart and looks real close at each piece but it cannot ever put things together. If you stay in the rational hemisphere too long everything seems totally depressing. The right hemisphere has to relinquish control so the rest of the brain can put it together and come back into the real world, not the thinking world. We have to pay a lot of attention to not staying in the rational hemisphere too long.

CEREMONIAL CIRCLE: What would you say to people who are just beginning to think about creating circles, doing ceremonies, connecting to the earth? What would you tell them?

Dolores: A lot of people who are just thinking of getting started have no friends to do it with. They just know they need something and they have some kind of a feeling they need ritual, but they have nobody to start it with. I'm talking about really beginning. Once you begin, people turn up that want to do something with you. I say a way to begin is with the sun, some sunrise, or some sunset. Get a piece of music which works; I use a Peruvian-Andean flute record. I'm not talking about real meditation music or music to put you in another state of consciousness. Usually some Native American flute music or music of a really landed people is best. Have that in your tape cassette every morning. Then, as you get up, watch when the sun starts rising and turn the music on and just watch the sun rise, being careful not to look directly into the sun as it can severely damage the eyes. When it finishes rising, turn the music off. Doing that every day is a real centering focus because you and the sun are communicating. You can do that even if you are in a city. It's hard, but even in a city the sun is going to move its rising point along buildings, up buildings, down buildings, behind a tree.

When beginners are trying to do rituals they are sort of uneasy. You think it might be fakey and you don't know when to start. Even if you're by yourself for full moons, that's really easy too because you just go out, preferably where the moon rises over something natural, and just watch it rise, start from there. This can be real good with even two or three people. The group goes out silently and walks. It's important to walk without a sound to the site where you're going to watch the moon rise and to watch it in silence. At the moment the lower rim clears you can all start chanting or drumming. That's a real good way to start.

CEREMONIAL CIRCLE: So in this case it's the sun or moon that really does it.

Dolores: It starts as the sun comes up. It takes a lot of anxiety away when you've agreed ahead of time what you're going to chant when you're first beginning. When the moon's lower rim clears, you all start chanting, then you're there. All of a sudden you're doing it.

CEREMONIAL CIRCLE: There's another kind of circle I'd like to speak to you about a little bit and that's the cycles. It seems to me that relating to that cyclical earth energy has a lot to do with connection too.

Dolores: When you settle into a place you can begin by setting up a henge.

CEREMONIAL CIRCLE: What is a henge?

Dolores: A wood henge is about the easiest one to do. Stonehenge is made of stone but you don't have to use stone. A henge is made to mark where the summer solstice sun and the winter solstice sun will rise next year. The sun will rise the same place on both equinoxes because they're the same time.

If you've got dead trees standing around, cut one and at winter solstice time plant it so that it creates a ledge that the sun sits on for three days.

At the end of its cycle the sun's movements are almost imperceptible and it will seem to rise at the same place for three days in a row. The sun will set right behind the post. It is very powerful to know it's going to do that. Then place one for summer solstice and you can go from there with as many more as you want. That's what all the ancient astronomical markers are. At Machu Picchu they were called the "hitching posts of the sun." Once you get hitched to the sun, your learning becomes very cosmic. Once you get a henge up, you'll be surprised at what can go on. People will go out and sit in the middle of it to meditate and watch how the sun moves and how the moon goes. The circle itself is a henge. The henge is a circle, so we're back to circles. It focuses energy for all the things that are going on. I think somehow energy builds up in the henge itself.

CEREMONIAL CIRCLE: You think the form of the circle builds energy?

Dolores: Yes and the fact that you're witnessing the sun and the moon going around in a circle is very powerful. It's your circle. You put it up.

CEREMONIAL CIRCLE: It's almost like that place becomes the center of the universe.

Dolores: Exactly. That's really true. In every people's culture, that was the center of the universe. That's where the sun and the moon circled around. The chant, I Circle Around the Boundaries of the Earth, was from Wovoka, the one who started the ghost dance for the Indians. It's Wovoka's ghost dance song. Well, there you are circling around the boundaries of the earth. It becomes more and more obvious to you that many, many things are included in your circle. As you're circling around, it becomes clear that your circle is much bigger than you thought it was.

There are four main festival days, the equinoxes and the solstices. In between, there are the cross-quarter days. Sonheim is an important day that we now call Halloween. It was the day the Celts brought the cattle in from the wild country close to the villages because it was going to snow pretty soon. When they brought all the cattle down into the main center, they had a big feast.

That was a very important day for the reconciling of the sexes. There's a god of the Irish called Dogda, "he who does everything right." He's the village god. On that day they would reconcile the wild goddess and Dogda. The male and the female energy would be reconciled over the fires.

The Yule, which comes later, is not one of the main cross-quarter days but in the Celtic tradition it is very important because it was the time they decided how much grain they had to carry the cattle for the winter without them starving. They would decide how much grain they had and if extra cattle had to be killed they had a huge feast.

The cross-quarter day in May is another time for male-female ritual. In the old days they went out to the woods and spent the night together. All the young girls and boys went out into the forest and brought flowers back and decorated this pole and danced around it. It was another reconciling of yin-yang energies.

When summer solstice occurs it is the height of yang energy, but at that moment, yin energy starts and it grows till winter. Then winter solstice is the height of yin energy and at that moment yang energy starts. There is no separation, no cutoff and that is important to realize. In a real culture there is only a cyclical progression. You go through the year and then you are back recreating another.

Most cultures had a world renewal ceremony to renew the world each year. The California Indians were especially strong on world renewal rituals. In southern California renewal time would be spring, when everything gets green after being so dry and in the north it might be sometime else. Every culture has a different time for world renewal. Here in Colorado it's when our ice melts. In some countries, it's when the fall rains begin.

Fundamentally, that's when everybody in the group puts out a lot of energy so the world can continue and if they don't, the world stops. In lots of different tribes the men, rather than racing one another, would all just run and run and run. That is giving energy to renew the world. Whatever time is chosen, a lot of activities are done at that time. It's to give energy to the world so it can continue another round. In the Indian pueblos they dance the other species. Somebody is a squash blossom, somebody is a deer and the deer speaks to you in the deer dance. That is how the other species help make the decisions.

At the world renewal rites at your place, you could start with an all-night trance dance. Then invoke the moon and, at the end of the time, have a talking staff where each person who had become the deer, or the redwood tree, would give their opinion of what's going on. I think this is a really good thing. It's workable but it takes a while to get started. The important thing is to get out of pushing the world around.

ANNA HALPRIN

It was a warm northern California August day as we drove through the redwoods to get to Anna Halprin's home on the slopes of Mount Tamalpais. She lives at the end of a winding street. There were a number of her students' cars parked outside along the road. We arrived a little early for the interview and went for a walk around the grounds. Below the house is a huge outdoor dance platform-deck with tiered seating on one side, surrounded by redwood and oak trees. Adjacent to the deck is an enclosed dance studio with no mirrors on the walls. Anna wants people to look within and join each other in the creative process. She believes everyone is a dancer and she lives her beliefs. She is an innovator in the use of dance and movement with interracial, multigenerational, and often untrained dancers.

Anna did New Age work before the label was popularized. She is passionate, articulate, warm, and friendly. We felt at home with her and were impressed with the depth of her knowledge. Her vision created a series of dances called Circle the Earth, in which communities, worldwide, simultaneously made a peace dance. In 1989 over three thousand people in thirty-six countries met and danced on the same day. This dance grew out of work that she was involved in called Search for Living Myths. Five women had been murdered on the hiking trails of Mount Tamalpais and Anna and her husband, Lawrence, gathered with others to respond to the situation. They chose to perform a dance to exorcise the mountain and reclaim it for the community. Many others joined them for a dance that was called In and On the Mountain. Soon afterward the killer was caught and peace returned to the mountain. And so this living myth grew in an ever-deepening and expanding vision. Some of her work now is devoted to creating dances to deal with the fear and suffering that AIDS has brought to so many.

Circling the Earth

CEREMONIAL CIRCLE: How do you use the circle in your dance work?

Anna: There are only two types of group dances, you either circle or you go in a line. The circle is an archetypal form in all cultures. In dance it's not only natural, it's what you automatically do when you want a group of people to come together. It's important in forming a circle whether the participants are facing inside or outside the circle, whether they're moving in or out, or to the right or the left. If they're facing into the circle, then all the people on the outside are excluded. The circle becomes sacred for what is inside.

When you visit the Pomo tribe, the first thing you do when you walk in the entrance is move in a small circle three times and then circle around the whole space, including the center pole, which is a circle. You circle three times and you make your own individual circle at two different points and then you make the bigger circle. What you're saying with your circling is that you're purifying yourself. "It's my own universe, and now I'm purifying the collective space."

There are many symbolisms around the circle. We're talking about the circle that you can create around yourself which is your universe, and the circle that you create with other people, which becomes the collective space. If you're circling to create a separate space inside, where you face is important. If you're creating a circle to send messages outside, then you must face outside, otherwise you're containing, almost trapping it inside.

One experience I had before we did Circle the Mountain came in relationship to the murders. There were five women murdered on these trails and I did workshops called "Search for Living Myths, Rituals through Dance Environment." We didn't know what the myth was going to be. We didn't know what story the community would select, only that we wanted to create something that was based on real-life issues, that was significant enough that it would not only require dedication and time but that, in the process of doing, would have as its purpose to create some desired change. In other words, we were looking for a way to find meaning in dance once again, content that linked it with people's lives.

When we did that dance people started drawing pictures of the mountain, and then suddenly everybody's repressed rage and feelings about the killer and the desecration of this sacred mountain began to be expressed. We began to realize that our feeling about this desecration would form the basis for the new myth we were searching for. We knew that we would create a dance and as a community walk up the mountain together.

We did a ritual dance in a theater at the foot of the mountain. I had stopped dancing in traditional theater spaces years ago, but somehow this building seemed like the appropriate place. I was concerned that it was a rectangular space and that it separated the audience from the performers. It had all the wrong symbology so I had to find ways to recreate the space differently. To do this we ran in a circle the entire time that the people were coming into the auditorium. It was a constant rhythm as we ran in that circle for over half an hour, and everything that happened was because of our running. We ran counterclockwise and then we ran clockwise.

Just before the performance one of the members of the company had decided to come running in down the aisle during the murder scene and enter the stage from the audience area. I felt a little uneasy about it but I didn't know why and didn't say anything. It was an interesting and dramatic idea and I didn't know why it made me feel uneasy until after it was done.

He came rushing down the aisle and the moment he hit the invisible circle which had been created by our intentful running, he fell and split his head open. I saw that we had established a strong circle, claimed it as our sacred space, and that this had created a very powerful force field. This was a very important experience for me toward understanding circles. I suspect that we had imbued the circle with invisible powers that hovered in the space.

It's your whole sense of intent about what you're doing in a circle that's more important than the circle itself. If everybody is facing in the same direction, and everyone is in mutual alignment about the purpose of their movement in that circle, and they manifest it in a rhythmic motion in which they surrender their own individual preferences, and they go for a common beat, and they say we are one and we're going to surrender all and yield to this common beat, and we're all going to do the same movement, and we all believe that by doing so something bigger than ourselves can take place, *then* you've got a powerful circle.

If your circle is facing inward what you're doing in that circle is making a certain statement. You are establishing a vortex of power that will come right up through the center and create a center pole in the circle. You can't see it but it's there.

In Circle the Earth we do that with sound. It's a series of expanding circles with the intent to create a vortex, like a peak that goes straight up, moves out, and spreads like a fountain. That's another way of using the center and again the intent is there.

We've had dancers in rainbow colors who ran facing clockwise, which is very different than facing out or facing inward. As they moved, their circle gradually spiraled out to the edges of the space, making a rainbow, the sign of peace. It says that our peaceful messages are going up to the heavens. We had four people walking in four directions saying that peace wasn't just spreading out, but it was going to all four continents, to all the peoples of the world—the black people, the red people, the yellow people, the white people.

Another dance that we do is an earth run. It's done with over one hundred people and is a mandala of peace. We make a small circle inside a larger circle, inside a still larger one. The inside circle needs to be large enough to allow for plenty of empty space. The people in the outer circle run clockwise and in the second circle run counterclockwise. The outside circle that goes clockwise is medium tempo. The center circle also moves clockwise and is slower because it's moving in less space. The circle on the outside is larger and faster. Actually the beat is the same but the step and the force is different. If you're going one way, at this tempo, it's one force, but if you're covering more space, at the same tempo, the force is different. If you're in the center the force is easier.

So you have three dynamics that make a conscious difference. What you're doing is giving rein to each individual to make the fullest commitment they can possibly make as they place each foot on the earth. If I'm a big person with large legs and I'm a runner I want to be able to make my fullest commitment in that circle. So I have to have more space. If I'm an eighty-year-old woman and I want to be part of this and I want to make my fullest commitment, then I want to be in the easier circle. You allow every person to put their fullest energetic force behind their movement in that circle to make their most powerful statement.

The danger of a circle is the danger that any unifying action has. Any unifying action has an inherent danger of wiping out the individual for the sake of the collective. As long as the individual can feel totally true to their own nature and their own unique vision, to that extent they can be creatively and peacefully engaged in a collective statement. Otherwise you have your gurus and your Hitlers. That's real important to me about circles because circles tend to create a lot of power that could be easily misused.

In this circle, within the three possibilities, everyone had to find their edge and then go past it. It isn't enough to be on your edge, or to go this side of the edge, you must go past your edge to make this kind of commitment.

When I talk about a circle I am also talking about the four points that create that circle. So in this dance when you are winded and you want to be part of the circle but can't physically stay connected, you choose to stand in one of the four directions and keep the pulse going, feel the circle moving and be part of it, because you're one of the connecting links that make the circle. I believe that the circle and the square, when they're overlapping and coming together, create a kind of ultimate geometrical form of harmony and balance. I also feel that the four points are inherent in a circle. That's how you get your sense of measurement about the circle.

A particular dance in Circle the Earth is made up of a series of circles. The first part of the dance is all in lines, forwards and backwards, and then other movements which are very helter-skelter, or movements that come up from the ground that are dispersed. The moment we went into a dynamic state of peace, everything from then on just automatically went into circles. There was no way of getting out of it. There was no way we could return to the linear form or to a scattered form. It seemed like the circle was the organic way of a group expressing a powerful image, both where they felt as individuals, reinforced by the group, and where they felt also part of a group, reinforcing a group spirit.

When we went up to the mountain to reclaim it after the dance was done we took about eighty people up. When we arrived, Don José Matsuwa, a hundred-year-old Huichol shaman, was there. He had felt some sort of call to come to this mountain at that particular time. He called it a sacred mountain.

When we got to the top we decided to circle around the peak before we walked down. Don José led us around the mountain and as he went around he would stop and tell us ancient stories about what had happened right here, and what had happened here, and what had happened there. Every time he stopped at one of the four corners he told of something special that had happened there.

The next year, inspired by Don José, we had seven different religious leaders who took us around the mountain, including a Native American, a Sufi and a rabbi, a priest and a Zen Buddhist. They all went around the mountain and said prayers at the four points. One spiritual leader would start with one prayer and then, as they went to the next point, another would add to that prayer. They kept adding to one another's ideas so that it made a collective idea. They took the feather of Goldie, a hawk, which had been carried by runners around the mountain. They all held the feather and made a circle with it. When I saw them do that very spontaneously I thought, that is the ultimate circle, because they've all come together in unity. They're standing in a circle in order to hold the feather which was in the center of the circle; they're all lifting their arms up and their hands are all touching, because of holding the feather. It's as if they are circling the mountain, in their own symbolic form there. It was as if they were creating a spiritual circle which had the spirit and symbology of the pyramid. Whenever you do an upward movement the feelings that are evoked are ones of aspiration, yearning, searching, seeking, ecstasy. For the circle to have this peak in it with their bodies rising up made it an ecstatic spiritual circle.

This feather has become a circular link, because it is now actually circling four continents. This circle has expanded from creating a small measure of peace on this mountain to moving out into the world, where circles are being created on all four continents and the feather is the link. The feather is the reminder that the circle was created here and has been created at the United Nations Plaza, and in Boston, and the American Dance Festival, and down in the Southwest. The circle's been done in the Pomo roundhouse with Native Americans. We weren't watching them and they weren't watching us. We actually danced together! We danced with the tribes in New Mexico. The circle has actually become a container that is bringing people together who would not have normally ever danced together. It's gone to Switzerland, where it brought people from Europe all together. I did Circle the Earth there right after the nuclear accident. That circle became a personal healing. It's become a healing circle between whites and Native Americans and a healing circle for the people in Europe, who were feeling totally frustrated and had no way to express their feelings of rage and helplessness.

The circle I described has gone or will be going to Australia and to twenty-five communities on four continents, to Japan and New Zealand, all of Europe, England, France, Germany, Austria, Poland. It's going to be done all over. It is our first planetary dance. It's grown from a very simple circle in a traditional theater, to the circle around the peak of our mountain, to all these international circles.

CEREMONIAL CIRCLE: Do you think there is a biological impulse to circle?

Anna: In all my years of working with large groups of people, no matter what I have done in terms of random movement, when people begin to feel a sense of group they will always start walking in the same direction, in a circle. You would have to set up a barricade to interfere with that natural tendency. Then there is a second tendency when the circle begins to come in to the center of the space. In other words, a sense of vortex seems to be biological. It's not unlikely because when you think of movement in the body it's circular.

All movement is rooted to circular action and it's in the anatomy of the body, in the joints. I suspect that's what manifests itself in space when you have large groups of people move back into circles. Even the musculature in the body is linked together through spiraling. Nothing is ever at right angles or lines, everything in nature has a piece of a circle in it, has a curve which is the essence of a circle. I think it affects our psyches that we're constantly moving in circles.

Brooke medicine eagle

We drove through the Sacramento Valley on the way to Joy Lake, a New Age healing and teaching center in the Sierras. The valley was smoggy and noisy, with miles of tract homes and gas stations. We came through the south side of Lake Tahoe at night and saw people inside the casino playing slot machines. It felt good when we reached the dirt road that led to the center. We slept in a pine grove near the Medicine Wheel and breathed the scented air.

In the morning we connected with Brooke's secretary. Our interview with Brooke would be held during the lunch break at her cabin. Sedonia went to her morning workshop, which was for women only. They gathered in a beautiful round yurt and about thirty women joined Brooke in the circle. She created a very beautiful altar with her pipe, many lovely feather fans, and a huge quartz crystal. The morning teaching was about singing and dancing and was almost entirely experiential.

When we arrived at her cabin she was resting on her bed. She looked beautiful, as though she had just awakened refreshed from a nap, even though she had just finished teaching for four hours. Her energy was straight, sincere, and passionately committed to her vision. She has a deep interest and respect for the circle. She understood perfectly what we were asking.

Brooke grew up on a Crow reservation in Montana and is a teacher, singer, and licensed counselor. She recently created a four-year cycle of large ceremonies to align the consciousness of people around the globe, with the purpose of clearing and healing unworkable personal patterns and to move us gracefully into a golden new time of harmony and peace on Earth. She has written a book, *Buffalo Woman Comes Singing*.

Dancing the Dream Awake

CEREMONIAL CIRCLE: Brooke, why do you do so much of your work and teaching in circles?

Brooke: There is a certain part of me that hasn't chosen it, it's very much part of my tradition to circle. One of the things that I'm being taught right now is that a lot of our work on Earth is about the principle of alignment. We must align ourselves with each other, and with larger and larger groups, in order to do anything.

When we think of lining up we normally think of a straight line that has a beginning and end. My teachers tell me that the most powerful line is a circle, where there is no beginning and no end. It is totally continuous. There is no leader and no follower and yet everyone is a leader and a follower. At the same time, if the circle is a true circle everyone can see everyone else and interact with everyone else. So there is the awareness and the ability to see and be with everyone. That is exactly what we are asked to do on Earth now. It is a perfect metaphor for us stepping into the greater circle of Life. Not only the greater circle of the other two-leggeds, but the even greater circle which is all of life.

I have heard it said that we two-leggeds are now maturing to step into that great circle. It is already functioning very well and harmoniously, but we haven't quite gotten ourselves in step. So we are being asked to step into that greater circle.

I work with the physical body to teach. The metaphor of moving and sitting in a circle is a learning that goes deeper than people know. We can be talking about almost anything while sitting in a circle and something is happening in the physical nervous system that isn't happening if we are sitting in rows and lines. It functions by itself, in a sense. There is a physical impact on the human system that happens whether or not people are talking about a circle or about oneness.

I'm working the circle sense of things back into meetings and gatherings so everyone can take their time and be able to speak as long as they want, going completely around and around and around until consensus is reached.

In many different aspects, from teaching, to meetings and gatherings and decision making, and political things, I think the circle is very useful. The more I know about it the deeper the teaching there is in it for me.

CEREMONIAL CIRCLE: So the circle is the teacher?

Brooke: I think so. There are new things coming to us about it, but we have just barely begun to touch the depth and possibilities of the true understanding of the cycling and circling of things. It is the teacher, and no matter who uses the circle, it is teaching.

If it is a circle, you really can't goof it up very much. It has its own integrity, its own form. There is something I get a kick out of doing. I'll say to people "Let's form a circle." They often have had nothing to do with a circle. If people can't actually get themselves into a circle and they don't really know what a circle is, how could they possibly understand the concept of oneness, of being in the great circle of things? I tease them, and say "You know, what we are going to do is spend the whole weekend figuring out how to truly get in a simple, round circle."

It is hard for some people. You can see ones that are standing inside the circle, or outside the circle, or they are backing out, or covering up someone. The understandings that you can gain from this are so powerful. I think the actual physical lesson that it takes to get yourself in a true circle is a part of building the nervous system that it requires to be in the circle of life. Whether it is the circle of your family, or your community, or your larger family of all of Earth's children.

CEREMONIAL CIRCLE: We usually think of human beings, but it feels like when you speak you are including all the other beings in a circle. Could you speak a little about that?

Brooke: I'm turning my work a lot more to being out on the land so that people can touch that circle, the larger circle of life rather than just their little life and the life of two-leggeds that we've formed in the cities. One of the strategies is to take people out to the larger circle of life, and then maybe we'll remember how to be a circle in our own family life as two-leggeds. That feels so important to me. Vision quests are good for that.

CEREMONIAL CIRCLE: I know you are doing a series of very large circles, now. Could you speak about that?

Brooke: If we are going to change from war to peace, from fear to love, that will require a total flip of the card. If we are going to make those incredible changes, from feeling inadequate in our bodies to the extraordinary miraculous powers that we really hold, it will really be quite a flip. If we're going to actually flip the card, the only way we can do that is by coming together in consciousness. For me that is represented as a large circle.

I agreed to a series of four ceremonies, or circles. We created circles to pray for the trees in the Amazon, and to help break the chains of family dysfunction and alcoholism. Those circles were very powerfully aligned in intent. We came together and cleared ourselves so that every step we danced was aligned. We were in fact a circle, there wasn't some kind of hanging in or falling out. We were doing one thing together, we were a circle in intent as well as in physical movement, dancing and praying.

We did Prayers for the Amazon in 1985, then we did the Breaking the Chain ceremony, really asking that all family dysfunction be cleared and changed and that a chain of love and light join us rather than a chain of dysfunction. Then there was a ceremony called Dance the Dream Awake.

We aren't really very good at circling, or at drumming and dancing, or at the whole cycle of ceremony. My people lived their lives in a ceremonial circle and were very good at it, the logistics, the food, the place, the whole thing. We need to practice and get better at it, with more and more people willing to do it. We are just babies, but there is so much possibility for circle after circle.

I have a lot of gratitude to my native elders. Dancing in circles, going into sweat lodge, all of those things were banned and people were killed who tried to hold these simple beautiful ways. My gratefulness is to those who had the heart and courage and love and spirit to bring those things to us. We are babies just beginning, but the knowledge is ancient in our bodies. We are just remembering.

It is exciting that as we put the word out people all over the world are joining the larger circle. We are holding the center, in a sense. That larger circle begins to include circles and circles and circles, all in a larger wheel, and that begins to make something powerful. Our elders tell us that as a certain percentage of the human population aligns with one another and joins together in consciousness, the card will flip.

Let's say we are all on a card. Some people gather in one spot and get a little group and do it their way, and some people jump up and down and try to be real active and flip the card that way. Some go over and hang over the edge and almost drop off, and some do drop off, trying to flip it that way. This is the way we are doing it now. The way it will work is when enough of us get together in consciousness, in one corner of the card, align ourselves, and all jump together. That will flip the card. The larger circle is both what we need and what we are wishing for. It is both the solution and the new dream.

White Buffalo Woman came and brought the sacred pipe to the Lakota people. That pipe is the representation of the oneness of all things. She brought the pipe of oneness and said that it was to teach and remind us of that oneness, being in the great circle, really standing together in that circle and recognizing and respecting each other and all things on Mother Earth. To me she is saying that we who stand in that great circle will pass through into a new time.

I think White Buffalo Woman is calling in her accounts. Are we one with each other or not? Are we even talking about it, or if we are talking about it, are we doing it? That is certainly a great circle She is talking about. A circle with all things dancing together.

My teaching has been that through our belly, through our actual physical center, our womb in women, our belly, that spot a few fingerwidths below our navel, is where Mother's mind lives in us. If we think of an umbilical cord connecting us to Mother Earth, just like an umbilical cord connecting you to a mother, it is very obvious that through that same cord we are connected to everything else Mother is connected to. All of her children, everything, whether it is the rocks and the trees or the elk or the winged ones. We are connected through our belly, through our womb, through that great circle that is our center.

I think we are going back to that. We are going back into the womb of Mother to feel her. We are stepping back into the circle in so many ways, into the womb, into that round, beautiful place that brings us back to the center of things.

CEREMONIAL CIRCLE: So the belly is one way into the circle?

Brooke: I think so. I think it's odd for most of us to feel that, because we were taught so often that because of sexual feelings and other things we were not supposed to feel our belly. We are not supposed to feel anything below the belt, and we have cut ourselves off. We've numbed ourselves out. Women have tightened their bellies to hold them in so that they don't hang out and look unattractive, or they have tightened them to keep themselves pure. We have literally cut ourselves off from our bellies. We have cut ourselves off from Mother, because that is where she lives within us. That is where our connection is.

Once we can feel our belly, and feel our connection as it comes out of our belly, the connection with the trees, for instance, will be different than an intellectual one. It will be something different than thinking about them in a good way. It will be, "For heaven's sake, *no!* Those are our family, those are our people . . . that is our circle."

The wonderful thing about dancing in a circle is that if someone slows down, if someone falls, or gets out of place, it throws the whole circle off. We need that lesson in our lives, and as we do more of that we understand that if we knock someone out of the circle and they fall, then the whole circle is affected.

That makes me think as well of pollution. The Chernobyl experience and pollution in general is like a negative circle. Now we understand that it isn't just Chernobyl or Three-Mile Island that is affected. It does go around the circle. I hope that the learning we can get out of that is that we need to send some positive things around the circle.

White Buffalo Woman's pipe law has taught that anything we do to any one of Earth's children, we do to ourselves. We are actually starting to get that, although we've had to do it in less than positive ways. As we understand that it just makes obvious sense to give away good things, to give away love and caring and aliveness, life and joy, rather than to give away death and destruction.

At one time what I was seeing and hearing from Mother Earth was that there was a good possibility that she would be eliminated as a place to learn and be. We were just so far off and out of balance that we'd just have to blow the whole experiment. What I am hearing now is that Earth will remain, and those who are willing to be in the great circle of harmony will remain. The Earth will be a place of harmony. The great circle will be evident, and that dream will be awake on Earth.

I think there is a lot more shaking going on than we even realize, and when peace finally dawns on us and we are willing to accept it and bring it into ourselves, we will just be stunned at what we were doing, how much there was that was happening and how crazy and out of balance and bizarre it was.

There are a lot of people talking about an axis shift and I have such a strong sense that dancing and circling will have a powerful influence on that, because we are speaking to Mother through our feet.

One of the fun things that we have found happening is that really large earthworms, about a foot long and three-quarters of an inch thick, are coming up when we dance! So you know there is something going down into Mother. Dancing in those circles we are communicating something. Hopefully there will be more and more communications of love and connection that may make some difference.

There is another kind of a circle that is very interesting. What we are starting to know more and more about is the saying: "Whatever goes around, comes around." Whatever we do creates something out there which then comes back to us. The way I am seeing it is that it goes faster and faster. What I do doesn't take ten years to come back to me, it takes ten days, or ten minutes. So it is speeding up, and speeding up, and speeding up.

The circle has tightened and I've realized that we really can't go on until we heal. If we have all of those issues from early childhood and they aren't resolved, they will just get worse and worse and life will be a mess. We can't just function and be happy on the surface and have that buried down there. It is like something is festering and it is breaking. We've got to deal with all those things. Whatever doesn't work is going to come around a hundred times worse the next time around.

I am such an optimist I like to think that we can move on and that is why it feels so strong for me to get out there and do some positive things with dancing and circles and getting people to just get the dawning in their minds that there might be another way to create and renew life rather than struggling and hassling with each other and fighting. We don't get what we need out of life, even though we think we do, by pushing and struggling and working hard and stressing and straining ourselves. How we get it is by dancing and praying and getting ourselves in that circle of harmony.

I feel powerfully called to get circles going, to get dances going. I feel that once people start dancing, they get it. I could say it a million times and they wouldn't experience it like they will when they actually get their feet in that circle and dance. Something deeper teaches them better than I could possibly do. It feels really strong now to be creating those because it is so easy to be problem-oriented. When we are cleaning up our old stuff we can spend all our time focusing on that, and we wouldn't know what to do if peace came. We wouldn't know how to be peaceful, to relax and be easy and love and care about each other.

I do believe that as we dance together in circles, sing and come together in celebration, that is the way we will renew our lives. We need to start doing it now. That will not only be a peaceful way, but it will promote a peaceful way. It will promote an understanding of what the possibilities are as we awaken ourselves in a golden dream of peace and a beautiful life on earth.

CEREMONIAL CIRCLE: What I hear is that the jump that is going to flip the card is a jump of joy.

Brooke: Yes! That is wonderful, thank you for that! That is wonderful because it is so true. I was told by my elders one time: "All you need to do is to experience joy." I thought: "Ah! That's a great assignment, that is so easy." Well it is pretty obvious that it isn't a very easy job. For me, that is what our new time will be, literally dancing for joy, singing for joy. You know when you think of joy, you're singing and dancing, jumping up and down for joy.

In our culture, laughter and lightness have been put on the bottom of the heap. If you are laughing, you are not doing right, you should sit down, shut up, and act right. It is not valued. Among the Lakotas the fourth great power (there was a power that created the world, a power that lives in everything, and a mysterious power of the East that is harder to describe) is Heyoka, lightness, laughter, coyote, the spin. It is like flipping the card, getting laughter and lightness and joy back on top. It is hard to believe it is such a challenge, but it is.

CEREMONIAL CIRCLE: What advice would you give to people who live in an isolated community, want to start making circles, and have no one there to teach them?

Brooke: I know that it is difficult because people feel that they don't know anything about it because they haven't done it. One suggestion is to find a deep understanding in yourself that all things are in circle. Just start looking around and knowing that circles are natural. Begin to feel the circles around you.

I have a sense that something very positive would be to reach out to the wider community and call in someone who dances in circles or does something in circles. Once you have danced in a circle, once it becomes obvious that it is so easy, that breaks the barrier. You know you can get people together and do simple circle dances. Many eastern Europeans have done folk dance. My Israeli friends do these wonderful circle dances, so it doesn't have to be a Native American dance, but any kind of dancing in circles.

These three things—observing nature and the natural circles, possibly calling in someone who will get them started, and then finding their own traditions and roots, circling and dancing—would be a beginning.

SEVEN

CIRCLE STORIES

DESCRIPTION OF CIRCLES FOR THE PURPOSE OF HEALING, REJUVENATION, CELEBRATION, AND PROTEST

We formed the circle, we danced,
we spoke the truth, we dared to live it.
STARHAWK

At the heart of every viable culture and community are groups of people who gather together to share their creative energy. This has always been the way on this sweet earth, only now we live in a global community that must begin to communicate cohesively to create a new paradigm for survival on the planet. A highly evolved communication grid has given humanity the potential for transiting the global crisis and has greatly expanded the opportunity to find the oneness of life. This really is a time to think globally but we need to establish circles on a local level for that potential to be realized. The vision is of a grid of strong, place-based circles networked around the planet.

We circle to find our way back into a sense of community, but now the community is larger. We circle for the seasons, that the cycle of life might continue; to honor the four quarters of the solar cycle, that the sun be respected as the best source of renewable energy; we circle to honor and defend our rights and the rights of those who have no voice; we circle to honor our life transitions, as we wed, give birth, bless, and heal one another.

Sometimes we simply circle to celebrate the joy of being alive by drumming and singing together. There are times we circle separately as women and men to share our concerns and joys about being women and men and other times we circle together to better understand each other. We circle to practice authenticity so we can speak the language of the heart, be witnessed and heard by those willing to listen with the ears of the heart.

The following stories are examples of a few of the ways and places in which circles happen. There are as many ways to make a circle as there are people to make them. It is our hope that these stories will inspire you to find your own circle way. These experiential stories come out of many years of circling.

Sedonia is part of several ongoing circles that meet at varying intervals. She belongs to a women's lodge that meets twice a month; to another lodge of women who are preparing themselves to become wise women elders, which meets four four-day weekends a year; she co-leads, with her partner, larger ceremonial circles; she sits in circles with questers out in the desert eight times a year; and she belongs to several other lodges that meet to explore issues and psyches.

Joshua is part of an ongoing men's drumming circle, drums for a circle of midwives, and is a part of a circle that drums at major festivals that meet in California and Oregon.

FAMILY CIRCLES

The people in your life that you feel closest to and the most open with are your family. It is wonderful when this family includes blood relatives but more often it becomes the people you have chosen to be with as an adult. The circles we have included in this section are ones that knit the chosen family together and bring dignity to the transitions of joining and separation, birth and death, the sharing of food and heart space.

Council Circle of Two

Two people sitting together with intention and commitment to the truth can constitute a circle. This is a technique that can be used by a couple, by friends, relatives, or business partners. It can be used when there is conflict, but is probably most effective when it is regularly woven into the lives of people who have an ongoing association. It creates a kind of time-out and makes space for the sacred to enter everyday life.

My partner and I, Sedonia, sit in council together once a week. We

Parents and children form a circle on the beach.

set aside a time and a space that won't be violated or interrupted. We place a special rug in front of a small altar that contains things that are special to our relationship. We begin by smudging one another and the altar, then we light the candles. We use a feather or stone as our talking staff, unless the issues involved are big and then we use our marriage bundle.

This is the time when we can each speak whatever is on our minds, knowing that we are in sacred time and space together and the other is obligated to listen with an open heart and to respond in truth. We stay with the issue until we have both really heard the other and owned whatever feelings come up.

Sometimes we have hard and difficult things to say to one another, but most often we use the time to tell the other how deeply we care and how much we appreciate the gifts they bring. Whatever the content, this circle always brings us closer and into a deeper seeing and knowing of the other.

I have used this form when planning a workshop with a friend, beginning a business relationship, or saying good-bye to someone I loved and wouldn't see for a very long time.

Drumming and singing in a circle with children in a public school.

We recommend that our vision questers use this circle when sharing the deep experience of their quest time with a partner or special friend when they return home. It brings the listeners into sacred time and space so they can hear the sacredness of the story and find their own threads to it. It can be used in sharing an experience that you feel needs to be heard in a special way.

Baby Blessing Way

A blessing way is a ceremonial gathering held on the new moon just before the scheduled birth of a baby. Both women and men can be invited, although sometimes only women are included.

On a warm, sunny day in June a group of thirty people gathered on a secluded part of a California beach. The gathering included friends of the expectant couple, several midwives, and about a dozen children who played and swam as the adults formed their respective circles.

The mother-to-be and the other women sat together on the warm sand

Parents-to-be with a circle of friends in a Blessing Way ceremony. *Photo: Suzette Buroughs*

in a large circle around an altar made of things that were of significance to the mother. After four women, each sitting in a different direction, had called in the power and blessing of her direction, the group began to drum and sing. The women were encouraged to sing songs that would have special significance to a soon-to-be birthing mother. While the singing continued the midwives placed a large bowl filled with warm water, flowers, and sweet herbs in front of the mother. With great tenderness they began to wash and massage her feet, and afterward to dry them with cornmeal that had been blessed by the grandmothers.

The mother of the mother-to-be brushed her hair, arranging it in an unfamiliar way to signify the changes that were about to occur in her life. A blanket was spread in the center of the circle and the young mother was asked to lie on it. All the women came forward and surrounded her, each placing their hands softly on her body and rocking her gently as they chanted *om*. Then all the women returned to their places in the circle and a talking staff was passed. As each woman held the staff she spoke her prayers and blessings for the new family and presented the mother with the gift she brought for the baby.

The men's circle was very different. They met about thirty yards away and there were fewer of them. They held hands in a circle for a few minutes but the expectant father, sensing discomfort among some of the men, decided not to have formal ritual and instead began to talk about his relationship with his father and his hoped-for relationship with his child. Though not going around the circle in a sequential way, all the men spoke and shared their experiences as father and sons. One man's father was dead and he spoke longingly about him. One young man had never seen his father and spoke of the emptiness which that brought him. The circle ended, as it began, with the men holding hands. While holding hands the father offered a prayer for his child-to-be and asked his brothers to join him with their own silent prayers. The men were not uncomfortable any longer as the circle broke and they joined the women.

When the women and men joined there was an awkward moment as couples decided whether to stand next to their respective mates. Some needed to accentuate their individuality, others rushed to hug one another. After a few minutes of chatter they began to sing a song that formally closed the circle. Then a potluck feast was spread on a picnic blanket and everyone ate, laughed, and enjoyed themselves.

Introducing Newborn to the Spirits

A couple with a new baby called a circle to honor and name her. They waited until she was ten days old because they believed it took that many days for a newborn to become firmly established in its body. It was a circle of ten women and men held outdoors in a beautiful setting. After making the circle and smudging, the parents spoke her name out loud for the first time. Then one of the men held the baby up toward the east, addressing the spirits and asking that they give their gifts of vision and inspiration, then holding her up to the south he asked that these spirits bring playfulness, joy, and open-heartedness; from the west he asked that she be given opportunity and the courage to know herself, and he asked the elders of the north to protect and guide her. He also introduced her to the earth and the sky, asking for their blessings.

Everyone in the circle sat down and a talking staff was passed so that each person could say a word of welcome to the new member of the community and a prayer that her earth walk might be one of beauty. A song was sung for her and there were gifts.

This child had heard the sound of drumming and praying while she was in her mother's womb and has participated in many ceremonial circles. She is now four years old and has a deep respect for the circle. When she is assigned a ceremonial function she does it very earnestly and gracefully. It's very important that children find their places in the circle and not just be brought to circles and allowed to be disruptive.

Food Blessing Circle

> In all you do, wherever you are
> do yourself and all life just honour.
>   William Blake

Our relationship to food is de-sacralized when pesticides are used that poison the air and water, when animal life is taken in cruel and inhuman ways, when farm labor is paid slave wages. Current agricultural practices consume more energy in the production of food than the food provides. That is a violation of sacred law. We can never be really nourished by eating such food.

When we honor the give-away of food it is a way to bring ourselves into gratitude and into mindfulness of its mystery. When we really understand ourselves as part of the sacred law of reciprocity, that that which eats is later eaten, we begin to see that to eat is a sacred act. This is a mystery that we need to reclaim.

Each time we break bread together it gives us an opportunity for making a circle. It is a time to thank the earth and all the people whose efforts went into providing the food. One of the purposes of circling around food is to empower us to take more responsibility in creating an organic culture. It is a form of circling that is easy to involve the whole family in.

Food Blessing

> I send my prayers of gratitude to all that has given of itself for this meal.
>   The strong beans, and the hardy grains, the beautiful leafy green plants and the sweet juicy fruits, I know you as my brothers and sisters.
>   I thank the sun that warmed and vitalized you, just as it does me, and the earth that held and nourished you, as it does me, and the waters that bathed and refreshed you, as they do for me.
>   I thank the fire that transformed you, just as I wish to be transformed by the fire of Spirit.
>   I thank the hands that grew and prepared this food, just as I thank all the hands that have touched me in so many ways.

Small Wedding Circle

This wedding was to be small and simple, including close family members and a small group of friends. It was held indoors in a lovely round building. Chairs were placed in parts of the circle for the older family members, and cushions were placed for others to sit on the floor. The bride and groom entered the room from the north and sat together in the south, facing an altar that contained things that were sacred to them. Guests were smudged as they entered the room and found their place in the circle.

The couple greeted their family and friends and thanked them for being present. The couple who were to officiate sat on either side of the wedding couple and one of them spoke a wedding invocation, explaining what the ceremony meant and asking for all present to bless this couple and their loving commitment to one another.

The directions were invoked by four friends and another led two songs. Everyone present joined in the singing.

> We are opening up in sweet surrender
> To the numinous love light of the One
> We are opening up in sweet surrender
> To the numinous love light of the One
> We are opening we are opening
> We are opening we are opening
>
> Let the way of the heart let the way of the heart
> Let the way of the heart shine through
> Let the way of the heart let the way of the heart
> Let the way of the heart shine through
> Love upon love upon love
> All hearts beating as one
> Light upon light upon light
> All shining through upon you

One of those officiating held the wedding rings and spoke of their meaning, then passed them around the circle so that each person could give a personal blessing to the rings and to the couple. Some of the blessings were silent, some came as songs, prayers, advice.

Then the couple faced one another and as they placed rings on each other's finger they spoke of their love and commitment, about what they brought to the marriage and what they were offering of their spirit to the other. They thanked the circle for being witness to their joining.

A member of the circle then led the group in a Sufi circle dance that involved opening and sharing heart-space between all present, to the song:

A circle of two making their wedding vows within a large circle.

> May the blessings of the Goddess rest upon you
> May Her peace abide in you
> May Her presence illuminate your heart
> Now and forever more

The group moved back into the circle, the directions were thanked and dismissed, and everyone went into the garden for refreshments and celebration. The sweetness of this ceremony touched all present in spite of the differences of age, life-styles, and belief systems.

Large Wedding Circle

> We are a circle within a circle,
> With no beginning
> And never ending.

My partner, Bird, and I sent out the call to friends and relations to come witness and celebrate our wedding. Because so much of our connection has to do with our work together we were also asking our community to bear witness to our dedication to our path and our desire to serve the people.

A large wedding circle on the rolling coastal hills in northern California.

We held the circle at a beautiful rural community, with rolling hills and a view of the ocean. It was a perfect day with a slight breeze to cool the August sun. The guests met in a wooded area and many people joined with Joshua in the drumming. When everyone was assembled they formed a procession to walk up to the large meadow that had been marked with poles in each of the directions. Each pole was decorated with ribbons and flowers in the colors appropriate for that direction.

The procession, following Joshua and his drum, entered through the rustic archway in the east that had been decorated with flowers and ribbons, formed a large circle, and to the continuous drumbeat everyone in the circle was smudged with sage and other herbs, blessed with cornmeal and water.

Bird and I had been in an area nearby doing our own private ceremony and waiting to be called to the circle. We approached the circle feeling the excitement of the drums and our circle of friends, some of whom we hadn't seen for years. We entered and stood in the south, representing the openness of heart and the trust we were bringing to this union.

As we stood there in the south a woman sprinkled golden cornmeal entirely around the circle of one hundred and sixty people, declaring as she did that this was the wedding band, the ring that held each of us inside as members of this community, connecting all of us in overlapping circles. Then the two of us stepped into the center of the circle and knelt on the buffalo robe that had belonged to our elder, representing the spirit of the give-away, and together we created our Marriage Bundle. In it we each placed four things that represented the commitment and intention we bring to this marriage. We certainly could have done this alone on the beach somewhere but it seemed important to ask our friends' witness, to ask them to see that our intention is very strong and clear and that when needed we wish to be reminded of that intention.

After the bundle was made it was passed around the circle so that everyone there could add prayers and blessings, further empowering it. As it was being passed different people stepped forward and gave us special blessings. Some danced, some sang songs, some recited poems they had written, some gave prayers.

When the bundle returned we were escorted to the northern gate and the buffalo robe was wrapped around us, representing the commitment we were making to our community and our path. Then we moved to the eastern gateway and holding our hands together we made an archway for our family and friends to move through, thus giving our blessings to each of them. As they passed through they all stood on either side of us and holding hands they created a long column for Bird and me to pass under, and we received blessings in turn from all of them. The day ended with food and music and dancing.

Our intention for the bundle is to keep it on our altar and to open it from time to time, perhaps to place new things inside when we feel the need to strengthen our bond, perhaps to remind us of something spoken that we had forgotten. Perhaps most importantly, the bundle will remind us of the absolute openness and vulnerability we felt in the center of that loving circle of co-hearts, all witnessing our deep and total commitment to one another and to life itself.

Separation Circle

A couple invited some of the friends who had attended their wedding to help them with their separation. Though not legally married, they had lived together for five years and had a child together, the first for both of them. There had been good times and difficult ones and now they both agreed it was time to separate. Because they were part of a community, they understood that their separation would have an impact on their friends and it needed to be handled in a conscious way.

They did not want or expect anyone to take sides. They wanted to move into the next phase of their lives as friends and allies and both desired to remain part of this community. It had taken a great deal of work and goodwill to come to this together.

The circle was formed with drumming and singing and the directions were called in. The couple was then accompanied by a friend into the center, where they sat on a blanket that had been used in their wedding ceremony. The friend tied their wrists together with yarn and moved from the center of the circle. It was time for people to speak.

The talking staff was passed and people validated their personal relationships to them as a couple, how they had appreciated them, what good parents they were. The couple each spoke words of validation to one another, then each told the other and the circle that it was time to end this marriage and the reasons why. Naturally the couple had said these things to one another but it was important to state it within a witness circle. The people in the circle were asked to share their feelings about this separation and asked to find the place within themselves that could agree with the rightness of it. When agreement was reached the friend who had tied the couple's wrists together took a knife and cut the cord.

The level of emotion was very intense and someone began to sing and the group joined in a chant that lasted a few minutes. Then all of the members of the circle were asked to speak about the relationship they would have with these people who were no longer a couple. The two in the center spoke to the circle and then to one another about this new phase of their relationship and how they would cooperate in the raising of their child. They thanked the community for the support and encouragement that had made this separation ceremony an empowering act for all of them. Then they walked to separate sides of the circle and everyone held hands and chanted. After the powers of the directions were thanked the circle broke and there was food and dancing.

This couple's child was too young to be part of this circle but we believe that this would be a powerful circle for the children of a separating couple to participate in when they are old enough to understand.

Fiftieth-Birthday Circle

When a friend of ours recently turned fifty she invited lots of friends to celebrate with her. When it was time to form a circle she asked the people to arrange themselves according to how long they had known her. Her mother stood in the south, next her brother and sisters, and the circle formed. The celebrant asked that the people in the circle tell how long they had known her, the circumstances of their first meeting, and a few words about their current connection. Her mother spoke first and the talking staff moved around in chronological order. The circle included her siblings, children, ex-husband and lovers, people she had worked with in the past, the man she lives with now, and a lot of people who were new in her life. It was interesting to see the progression of her story and we all left feeling we knew her better.

Death Circles

Death happens at all stages of life. It can be reclaimed as a time of transition that brings the community into a closer and deeper relationship. The purpose of the ceremonial death circle is to release the spirit, to heal the loss to the community, and to celebrate the beauty and mystery of death. Just as we reclaim the mystery of sex and birth, we form a strong intention to honor all the transitions inherent in incarnation, including the disembodiment of Spirit.

We have included the story of an elder who lived a full and creative life and a middle-aged woman who died from a debilitating disease.

Elder's Memorial Circle

We both knew and loved Grandpa Roberts. Grandpa's greatest delight was to play Santa Claus at the local Christmas craft fair. His long white beard was real. He was a huge man, a blue-eyed mixed-blood with deep ancestral ties to the Cherokee people. He spent the last years of his life living in a little dome on the rural property of a world-known herbal school. He was self-sufficient up until the end. He was purported to be in his nineties and was so hardy that he took ice-cold showers on his outdoor deck every day of the year.

Lots of people followed the deer trail to his cabin and sought his advice, which he freely gave. He was always deeply involved in a healing process with many people. He always said that he was ready for anyone or anything that came down his trail.

A public memorial for him was held on a warm August afternoon. A large circle assembled around an open fire in a big clearing. The spirits of the land were present. After the directions were called in and some prayers were made, everyone was given the opportunity to come up individually to the fire and place something into it that represented Grandpa, or his or her relationship to him. In this way we were saying good-bye to him and releasing his spirit.

This was a deeply personal time for everyone who went forward. There were tears, and even occasional laughter when someone's good-byes reminded us of the humorous side of Grandpa. This weaving together of emotions made his presence seem very real in this circle.

As the last person was saying farewell, everyone in the circle gasped as a small whirlwind appeared from nowhere only a few inches from the fire and moved out through the eastern gate of the circle. We all knew that Grandpa had gone.

Simple Memorial Circle

She had lived a very simple and somewhat reclusive life. Her interests had been political in nature and she didn't come to a connection with Spirit until weeks before her death from cancer. Because of the kindness of a number of people she was able to die at home, cared for by friends, some who hardly knew her. She had asked one of them to be responsible for her memorial service and told him what she wanted.

She wanted it to be held on a beautiful piece of wooded rural property. About fifteen friends arrived to participate on a warm spring afternoon. They met in a circle and in the middle of it was a large bowl filled with her ashes and a vase of fresh flowers. She had requested some drumming and when this was done the group shared stories of how they knew her and what she had meant to them.

Each person was asked to take a large handful of her ashes and scatter them among the trees as he or she said final words to her spirit. When this was done the group gathered in a circle again and each person took a flower to carry home as a reminder to say prayers for this woman as she made her way back home.

INTIMATE CIRCLES—GOING DEEP

The circles in this section are examples of ways a small group of people can move into a deep place smoothly and quickly. They create a quality of interactive sharing that makes for a beautiful feeling of safe intimacy.

Circle of Stones

Our elder, Grandpa Roberts, always said that stones were the oldest and wisest people. He thought they could tell you anything you needed to know. This stone circle very quickly moves both the speaker and the others who are listening beyond their persona into a more transpersonal mode of being. This of course has the effect of drawing the circle together very quickly, of building a sympathetic bond between the participants and taking the group to a deep level.

Rocks of various shapes and sizes, colors and textures are arranged in a circle on an altar-cloth in the center of a room, either on the floor or on a table. Candles can be placed in the center and in each of the four cardinal directions. After the group of people has gathered around the circle of stones the candles are lit, calling in the power of each direction, and calling in the Spirit as the center candle is lit. The people are then invited to select a stone that speaks to them or that seems to represent something that they are feeling or experiencing at that moment. The circle members are then asked to feel and examine the stones they have selected. When they are ready they each, in turn, let the stones speak through them. They describe the stones and how they relate to their lives and issues, or to any particular issue that the group has decided to address.

When people are speaking they are allowed as much time as they need and no one is allowed to comment, interrupt, or ask questions. No one is allowed to play "therapist" for them or to fix things. People simply listen with their hearts, respecting the depth and the sincerity of the speaker.

This technique can be used when a circle is forming for the first time as a way of introducing the members to one another, bypassing the usual "My name is, I live at, work at, etc." It is an excellent way of getting people to examine their true intentions in joining the group. In an ongoing circle it is an excellent method for addressing an issue of real importance.

After everyone has spoken, the rocks that were chosen can be arranged into a smaller circle inside the larger one and a few moments can be spent in silent meditation in which the group holds hands and experiences the level of energy that they have generated by allowing the openness and vulnerability that this circle invokes. Then the candles can be blown out as each of the directions and the Spirit are thanked for blessing the circle and its process.

Singing Our Dreams Circle

Two evenings a month a group of friends gathers to share and explore dreams. They meet in a circle, sitting on the floor. After smudging one another they always begin with toning together to free their voices and to bring the group into harmony. When someone is ready to share a dream she or he moves into a special seat in the southwestern part of the circle and begins to sing her or his dream. One person drums softly and another rattles as the singer moves deeply into dream-space. It is not necessary to sing "well" to do this. The dreams can be sung in any way at all and the effect will be the same.

When the singer is finished a person designated as the dream-weaver asks the singer to sing the voice of different aspects of the dream. For instance, someone might sing a dream in which she or he is walking in the woods alone when she or he sees a flowered meadow in the distance, and as the singer approaches it there are birds singing. When she or he reaches the meadow there is a woman waiting and she beckons to the singer, and so forth. After the singer has sung the entire dream she or he will be asked to sing the song of the woods, then perhaps the song of the birds, the flowered meadow, the waiting woman. As the singer does this everyone joins in, each reflecting phrases and parts of the dream that seem the most interesting and vital to them. They are not allowed to interpret or to impose images that were not part of the dream singer's presentation.

This technique moves everyone in the circle into a space that replicates the trancelike quality of dreaming. In this manner the linear, waking-mind state is bypassed and the real feeling tone of the dream can be recaptured by the dreamer and experienced by the other circle members as well. In such a circle everyone makes the dream a part of their experience.

Hasidic Circle

A friend invited me, Joshua, to go hear Shlomo Carlebach. I had heard about him since his days in the Haight Ashbury where he started the House of Love and Prayer. Not only a singer, he has a repertoire of teaching stories that he tells for hours and hours and has been doing so with groups of people all over the planet for years. Once I attended one of these all-night sessions and watched him in action, keeping the stories alive.

Shlomo is a circuit-riding rabbi. On a typical day he would fly in from Paris to do Shabbas in New York and stay up all night with the stories, each one deeper, him crying, laughing, hugging the assembled. He would fall asleep at the table and seem to be soundly zonked, yet as soon as anyone would mess up the story, he would perk up, ask permission to correct them, and finish the sequence.

This event was in an upper-middle-class shul. It was not a very friendly crowd, although there were many present who loved and adored him. The host rabbi warmed the room up noticeably when he acknowledged Shlomo as a great teacher, one of his greatest teachers, and the man who had, almost single-handedly in the early days, stayed with his songs and brought more people back to Judaism than any one man. Shlomo has a way of speaking that many a Jewish kid who had been chanting Hare Krishna for a few months could understand. He knows how to be with the children of the sixties. He knows how to be with everyone.

It only took Shlomo a few minutes, singing and talking, to get everyone on their feet, circling around the huge prayer hall, dancing, skipping, hands raised, twirling. The differences between the people did not matter anymore; almost everyone got up on their feet. We circled around and around the hall; even the folks who sat in the rows smiled as they watched. An old woman who had not danced since she left Poland got up and when Shlomo saw her he danced out to her and held her with as much joy and delight as he held everyone.

Here is a man who, if I tried to explain to him about circles, would give me a pat on the cheek and not pay one iota of attention. He has no need for such concepts, they live in him by another name. I learned something very important from this, that a circle is possible anywhere.

Prayer-Lodge Ceremony

A women's lodge that had been meeting for about a year decided to invite the members of a group that had been meeting for six years to a prayer-lodge ceremony. The women in the newer lodge were nervous about their relative lack of experience and asked if the women in the older lodge would lead the ceremony. The women said no but that perhaps both lodges could do it together. When the visiting lodge arrived at the place it was to happen it was told that the inviting lodge had decided to be the leaders after all. The visiting lodge was pleased about this, feeling that the newer lodge was owning its power in a good way.

During the four rounds the form was held in a very feminine way because each round was led by a different woman and each woman's way was uniquely hers. Everyone got to experience a variety of energies. One round seemed loose and flowing, one was extremely intense and focused, one left space for a great deal of singing, and one allowed for a very sweet kind of verbal interaction between the groups.

We include this story to illustrate that there are many ways to do this work. Each of the women had gotten in touch with her own belly-wisdom and used that to create her part of the ceremony. There was no right way or wrong way, just her own unique way. The women from both groups did their part in keeping the energy good and on track and there was no competing for attention or authority. It was especially wonderful to be with people who could share their power with such graciousness and openness.

All-Night Singing Circle

Eight women sit inside a tipi. It is dusk on a chilly autumn evening. The tipi has been prepared and is very beautiful. The women arrange themselves around the center fire, each sitting on blankets and cushions that will help her stay warm and comfortable during the long ceremony.

One woman sings in the directions, another blesses the water, and another sages the space, the women, the altar, and the fire pit. One says prayers to the fire spirits and as the fire is lit the tipi begins to glow and dance in its light.

This is to be a singing circle and no words will be spoken. Some of the songs the women will sing will be known by everyone present and all will join in as she sings, other songs will be made up for the moment and the others will join in if the singer develops a refrain.

The first round of songs is dedicated to the ancient grandmothers, asking them to be present and to speak through each woman. The staff is passed and as one woman plays the drum and the others rattle, each woman in her turn sings her song to the grandmothers.

The next round is dedicated to the south and the songs are sung from the voice of the little girl in each of the women. Some of these are songs of pain and sadness, others are playful and silly. The next round are voices of the inner man and for this the west is invoked. These songs sometimes sound a bit strong and tough, sometimes halting and unsure, once or twice they bring gales of laughter from the group.

The next round is devoted to the north, the voice of the inner woman. These are songs of power, deep and revealing, and it seems as if each singer touches a part of herself she had hardly known before. For some there are tears, for all there is beauty. The next round is dedicated to the inner little boy, the spirit child, and during these the space begins to shimmer with excitement and electricity and the Spirit-connection is strengthened between these women and within each woman.

WOMEN'S CIRCLES

In 1968 I, Sedonia, took my sixteen-year-old daughter out of school and the two of us traveled and lived for two years all throughout Asia. We loved hearing the music, seeing the dance and the ceremony, the beautiful art of the people. But even more than that, we enjoyed watching the people, especially the women, as they engaged in the small details of their lives. We noticed the extreme care and attention they would give to the smallest tasks. We also noticed that the women would gather in small circles, laughing and talking and having a fine time as they worked. There seemed to be an aura of sacredness in these acts. No one seemed to be in charge. Some of the women were older and wiser and were sources of wisdom but there were no egos loudly demanding attention. We were witnessing woman's way.

So often when the anthropologists have reported on a culture they have overlooked the women's rituals. The women were so involved in

Women holding a garland in a circle at a Motherpeace Festival. *Photo: Vicki Noble*

A women's hair-washing circle expressing women's ways. *Photo: Elizabeth Cogburn*

weaving the everyday tasks, cooking, sewing, birthing, caring for the children, planting, with the sacred that the scientists simply did not have the eyes or the sensitivity to perceive it. It is reclaiming the sacredness of these small acts that will bring us to the realization that this entire earth walk is really a sacred dance and must be treated and honored as such.

The woman's way is one of being in nature, of dancing and singing, of loving and living joyfully. It knows that tears and laughter have equal value. It has the wisdom to listen to the inner teachings and those that come from the grandmothers. It is not afraid of the unknown. It knows that our dreams are our guides and that if we truly listen to them we can build a new way that is fair and just for all. It knows that if we separate our spirituality from our politics, and from our economics, and from our health care, and from our education, and from our food production and our child care, from our work and our play, we are doomed to fail at each. It knows that life can't be segregated and compartmentalized but is instead a dancing whole, each part depending on the others to give it integrity and direction.

Everyone-Makes-the-Ceremony Circle

At an annual Conference of Feminists in Psychology there was a circle that very much expressed women's ways. The two women who were in charge of this particular one-and-a-half-hour presentation were new to ceremony but they knew they wanted to be part of one. There were about thirty of us in the room and they divided us into six groups. Each group was given fifteen minutes to come up with a small ceremony that would involve the entire group.

The leaders had placed a beautiful cloth in the center of the circle and on it were candles, colored papers, plates with sand, cornmeal, feathers, seeds, glasses of water, sage, and flowers and we were all invited to use any of these things in our ritual.

The small circles were called back into the larger circle and each group, in turn, did the small ritual they had planned. Although many of the women in the room had never before participated in any self-generated ceremonies, each presentation was lovely and meaningful. Dancing, singing, chanting, praying, blessings, invoking, heart-opening exercises were all included. One group passed a large sheet of beautiful colored paper around and each woman was asked to tear off a piece in any way she wanted. Then we were asked to each, one by one, place our piece with the others in a way that interconnected them. It was a lovely piece of ephemeral art and touched everyone. Then we were invited to reclaim our pieces and take them home to place on our altars to remind us that our lives and our circles as women are interconnected.

I was especially moved by the spaciousness of the leaders who had completely placed the power in the hands of each woman present, trusting that if they just let go something wonderful would happen, and it did.

First-Blood Circle

Women's life passages are marked by blood: the entrance into adulthood that comes with menarche; the blood of birthing; the absence of blood with the onset of menopause. All are important rites of passage that were once a vital part of women's mysteries and women's power. Women are in the process of reclaiming these mysteries and are using the ceremonial circle as a tool for this.

Three young women in the community had all begun to bleed within weeks of one another. Their mothers and their mothers' friends decided to have a first-blood ceremony for them. There has been so much shame and secrecy for women about this very fundamental fact of women's bodies and these women wanted their daughters to have an experience that was positive and affirming.

The young women were a bit reluctant but when they heard that gift-giving was to be a part of the event their interest grew. The circle was held in the home of one of the women and twelve older women were there to honor and welcome the three young ones into the circle of women.

The sacred circle was established and then the older women each told the experience of their first menstruation. Although each story was different, most had experienced a difficult and confusing time, and each said that she wished a special circle had been held for her to help her more clearly understand this important rite of passage.

The three young women were given an opportunity to speak and to ask questions of the older women. They seemed very relieved to be given this opportunity and took full advantage of it. Then each woman gave a gift to each of the newly bleeding women, and with the gift offered her a special blessing and welcome into the sisterhood. More than anything else the older women urged the young ones to honor and hold sacred their femaleness and to treat their bodies as sacred temples. They also said that the young women could come to them any time for advice or for tea and conversation.

Everyone held hands and a prayer of gratitude was spoken in appreciation for being women and sharing this powerful time together.

No-More-Pregnancy Circle

Circles are used to honor difficult life choices. Several years ago a friend decided to undergo a tubal ligation. She was the mother of two teenage children and had made a clear choice that she did not want more children, and neither did she want to have an abortion. However, she was also very much in touch with what she would be losing through this decision. She came to me expressing the need to honor this difficult choice in a ceremonial way and asked me to help her. We sat together and planned a ritual that would include the grief of loss as well as celebrating the possibilities of other kinds of birth.

The ritual began with her going by herself into the woods for an hour while she made a small doll that represented the baby she would never give birth to. She took a diaper she had used years earlier with her second child and in it placed small objects she found in the woods, which represented all the things about motherhood she loved and cherished. She was menstruating at the time and she also put some of her blood in the bundle. She wrapped it to closely resemble a tiny baby and tenderly carried it back to our circle.

She told us about her "baby" and passed the bundle around the circle for each woman to cradle and admire. We each spoke to the baby bundle. Each woman related to the bundle in a different way. One woman who was the mother of two had passed through menopause, one woman in her early forties had made a conscious choice to never have children, one was an adolescent and had only recently begun bleeding, one had tried for many years to become pregnant but couldn't, another had given birth to three children and had made the decision to have a tubal ligation years before, and one woman had a small baby.

After we all shared our feelings about the "baby" and motherhood she built a small fire and carefully placed the bundle into the fire. As she did this all of us in the circle began to wail and cry, deeply sharing her grief and loss. A primal mother-response was touched in each woman present. The grieving continued for about ten minutes.

We formed a birth canal with our bodies and she crawled through it, each of us resisting her passage so that she had to struggle to be "born." Then we gathered around her, placing our hands gently on her body, and when she felt ready she spoke to us about the new things that were going to be birthed in her life now that her creative energy would be flowing outward rather than toward a child.

Three days later she went into the hospital to have her tubes tied and has not regretted the decision. She had deliberately scheduled the ceremony before the operation so she could be clear in her decision.

Grandmother Lodge

Menopause, when well dealt with, provides an initiation into personal power for women. Many cultures in the past have recognized this especially potent time, understanding that it marked a threshold and ushered women into the archetype of Grandmother, or Wise Woman. Contemporary society, fearing the Wise Woman's wisdom and not wanting to deal with her, has made such women virtually invisible, leaving many women feeling useless and impotent, leaving them to deal with the negative aspects of misunderstood menopause. The power released in women at this significant time in their life is often turned inward, resulting in many unpleasant symptoms, such as hot flashes, depression and mood swings, and a general feeling of being lost, unable to find a new and vital identity. The truth is that when women pass into and beyond menopause there is an opportunity to discover a deeper and freer experience of self.

In tribal times women who had passed into this phase of life were admitted into the Grandmother Lodge. In some tribes they said that once a woman had passed her "thirteenth moon-time," which meant that she had not bled for one lunar year, she was considered a wise elder and she would be expected to provide a voice of responsibility toward all the children, both human and nonhuman, to the earth, and to the Laws of Good Relationship. All tribal decisions had to pass through the close scrutiny of these tough and powerful older women who knew exactly who they were and what gifts they had to offer the people, women who were not afraid to say a strong *no* to anything that did not serve life.

This is a function that is left sadly vacant in contemporary times after thousands of years of patriarchal reign. The result is that we are on the brink of extinction and find ourselves living in a morass of dysfunction. We simply must recover this voice of the Grandmother. We need to claim the power and vitality of this stage of life and make our voices heard loud and clear.

I, Sedonia, was in jail for a week eight years ago because of a political action at Vandenburg Air Base. Many were arrested and all the women were placed in a large dormitory-style barrack. I found myself gravitating toward the older women. There were about seven or eight women in their late sixties and seventies who seemed to be the most interesting, wise, and fun-loving people in the group of over two hundred women. I was in my early forties at the time and this was quite an eye-opener to me. Later, when we all appeared in court and were given the opportunity to make a statement before the judge, I was quite moved by what happened. When Mary, an older Quaker woman, stood to speak she was so powerful and moving that the woman judge had tears in her eyes and the district attorney, visibly upset, abruptly left the room. Everyone in the courtroom was silenced by this small and powerful grandmother. I watched this being repeated as each older woman rose to speak.

Something clicked in me through this experience. I began to see that true power is earned through a long life, well lived. I saw that people will listen to older women when the women are ready to claim their wisdom and their right to speak it. To those women in prison it meant putting themselves on the line, being willing to take a strong stand in favor of what they felt to be right and ethical behavior.

Our first step in this is to claim power in the sphere of our own lives. This is work that younger, premenopausal women can begin at any time, and others who have been postmenopausal for years can claim as well.

As I grow older it is my experience that my life gets better and I feel freer and more authentic within myself with each day. No one had ever told me that this was possible and it has been an amazement and delight to me. I am also very aware of what has been lost. I miss the beautiful red blood flowing from me each moontime. There is an acknowledgment that I am growing older and that brings with it some fear, but also some excitement. There are ways in which I feel my life just beginning. I have been rehearsing for this part, for now I begin to really learn of wisdom. I feel like someone whose apprenticeship has begun anew, and in earnest.

It is time for older women to honor the possibilities of this powerful unfoldment with other women through heartful sharing, working through the process of grieving for what is lost when menstruation ceases, and creating meaningful ceremonies of initiation into the power and beauty of the Wise Woman time. It is necessary to work with the fears around growing old, being alone, unloved and unacknowledged, turning these fears into power.

Crone Circle

This is a circle of eight older women who are approaching or are in the midst of menopause. They agreed to come together one evening a week for two months to explore this important rite of passage. They began each meeting with drumming and casting the circle. A different woman agreed to lead each meeting.

One evening a woman led a storytelling circle in which each woman told the story of her first moontime, the time she began menstruating. The stories were sometimes beautiful, usually sad, and often funny. Everyone had brought a photo taken of herself at puberty to place on the altar. Another evening the group shared their grief about no longer celebrating the moon's tides with their blood, and their fears of growing old. There was relief when they heard their fears were very similar; looking old, being tired, aches and pains that come with aging, possible loss of sexuality, becoming invisible, being lonely and alone. There was healing in sharing these fears and having them witnessed and understood.

Another evening the women shared information about health issues, which herbs are helpful, the best diet to eat, supplements, exercise, natural sources of estrogen. One evening all the women made masks of themselves as very old women and the next week they wore them in the circle, allowing themselves to really experience being very old. They each told how they would like their old age to be, where they would like to live, who they would like to be with, and what they would do with their time. They made prayer bundles asking that their old age be good.

One evening they worked with death issues, using the time together to begin to face the inevitability of death. They each answered questions about how they would like death to come, how they would want their burial service to be, and what they believe happens after death.

On the last evening they designed a powerful ceremony into cronehood. They provided an initiation for one another that involved honoring what had been, what was being sacrificed, and claiming the power that was just beginning for each of them. For this circle each woman came in an old garment that she removed and burned, representing her old self, and replaced it with a beautiful new one that symbolized this powerful phase of her life. Each woman took a new ceremonial name that expressed her commitment to this exciting time.

The Spider Lodge

The Spider Lodge is a group of seven women who have been meeting for several years. Each of us leads a very busy life, as therapists, educators, and workshop leaders, and yet we are willing to set aside four days and nights, four times a year, to meet. The time together is very precious and is usually over before we have had a chance to say and do all that we want. In the beginning our reunion nights were chaotic, everyone having so much to share and catch up with. Sometimes it seemed as if the chaos at the beginning set the tone for the rest of the days together and a more sacred element was missing. To deal with this we created an opening circle that cuts through to the most essential part of each woman's story.

We gather at the agreed time the first night, ready to be in circle. We have arrived in silence and gotten ourselves settled into the environment. The room is smudged and a ritual is done, and then we move into the silent witnessing. When the first woman is ready, she enters into the center and begins to move wordlessly through her story.

Women creating an art project in a circle led by American healers in the Ukraine. *Photo: Patricia Waters*

One woman might have spent the past three months working very hard and feeling absolutely exhausted, and she will dance that. Another might have suffered a great loss or had a shattering experience and she will dance that. Another might dance the openness and excitement she has been feeling in her life and work.

When one woman was in the process of packing to leave the home she had lived in for many years she moved through her feelings and emotions in a way that was deeply touching. She had brought a huge packing box with her and placing it in the center of the silent circle, she got inside it and crouched very low. Garments, books, and other things began to be tossed out from the box. Most of us in the circle had begun to chuckle, when suddenly there was a wrenching sound. Deep inside the box she was tearing and ripping pieces of fabric, showing how her heart was being torn apart by this uprooting of her life.

I learned more of this woman and her experience in this moment than I could have ever known through words. We were all able to sit in witness, holding the feelings that came with the memories of all the times in our lives we had felt ripped apart.

During the days we spend together we do many things, most of it in circle. We often spend many hours a day in council together and usually as we speak on issues that are of vital importance to us at least half the members will be knitting or beading or doing something with their hands. This seems to bring a quality of embodiment and immediacy to the discussions. Topics that so often get moved into philosophical discourses in some groups seem to stay very grounded and applicable to life situations.

We had one of our quarterly meetings a few weeks before I was to be married and I asked the women if they would help me sew my wedding garment. It was one of the sweetest days of my life as I watched them work with the soft blue silk I had chosen. They helped me design it, then they cut and sewed it with beautiful, delicate stitches, each one taking a turn, as we held our council that day. It was finished when the last woman to work with it embroidered a tiny rose on a hidden part of the neck. Before my wedding I had the opportunity to get my sisters in another lodge to also add stitches as we circled together, adding their prayers. This garment was beautifully numinous after being touched and blessed by so many loving hands. This circle, more than any I had ever experienced, taught me something about women's way of making the small and mundane into something magical and transforming.

We are working together to become as clear and authentic as we possibly can, which involves the willingness to be very vulnerable. We have been learning to create a very safe container to explore issues of aging, of power and conflict, and of differences and how we deal with them. It is our intention to weave ourselves into a lodge that can express and walk Grandmother's wisdom in the world.

The Owl/Eagle Lodge

Once again the sun has set. The moon has risen and the air is full of magic. It is time to re-enter the dream. Time to re-enter the sacred womb of the mother.

Twice a month near the full moon and the new moon a circle of women meets in a small handmade house overlooking a wooded valley at the end of Owl Road. It is a circle of peers. The women meet for the purpose of celebrating their own as well as the moon's fullness, at other times to honor the emptiness that comes with the new moon that teaches them about the darkness of the void. The circle is a way of supporting one another as each steps closer and more fully into her own sacred and powerful circle of self.

The women arrive singly and in deep silence, pulled into the magic of the circle by the pulse of the large council drum that was handmade for the group. After all have arrived each in turn is smudged with burning sage, using feathers to spread the fragrant smoke.

As the drum enters and vibrates into the matrix of the circle, one woman will feel the impulse to allow a deep, primal sound to issue from her being, then another will answer, then another and another until a deeply moving conversation has been established. This may continue for an hour. Often because of tender or vulnerable places that have been touched the sounds turn into moans or wails, sometimes tearful sobbing. At other times they become laughter.

When this is finished the women may move into a muffled drumming and rattling and a verbal dialogue will be introduced by a member who needs an issue discussed in council. Becase of the strong, nonverbal, and heartfelt connection that has been established, and because the continuous playing of the drum maintains that connection, the women are able to discuss sensitive issues in a manner that is more devoted to truth and clarity than to smaller concerns. The sacred dimension that has been carefully established enables the women to speak and to hear from a deep and clear center that brings transformation for all present. The connection is transpersonal rather than merely personal. Often this provides an initiation into a totally new and more spacious seeing and experiencing of the world. This experience is, of course, carried by each woman as she leaves the circle, profoundly enriching the healing work that makes up the fabric of her life and all those she touches.

Because of an action contract I had made at a Long Dance ceremony, and in response to a deep need I was feeling in myself, I began a women's lodge. I had met in women's circles before. While living in Berkeley some years ago I had helped to organize a women's circle dealing with issues of creativity and focus. Six of us met for a year exploring the difficulty we had in putting our creativity out in the world and finding ways to stay focused on our work. The Creative Process workshops that I co-led for some years in the San Francisco area grew directly out of the work we did in that circle, so I knew the power of it. I knew I was ready for another push of creative expression and that I needed the support of sisters.

A friend and I invited women that we knew and respected and who were involved in various types of healing work, and eight women showed up at my house for our first full moon meeting. That night we drummed and spoke of our needs and visions and agreed to meet again. The lodge has changed and grown a great deal since that first night. Only three of those original women remain in the lodge. Women have come and gone and sometimes it looked as if we wouldn't survive, but we have. We have become a strong, cohesive group of nine beautiful and powerful women.

We decided on a few rules in the beginning. It was to be a closed circle of no more that twelve women. We would enter in silence and begin with drumming. We would find creative ways to use ceremony to honor ourselves and one another. It was not a place to come to gripe. Children, except for nursing babies, were not to be a part of this circle. Some of these decisions were, predictably, difficult to arrive at.

At first we met only once a month but soon found that wasn't enough to maintain continuity so we changed to twice monthly. One of our first projects was building a prayer lodge together. That meant collecting long willow branches, lots of volcanic rock, digging a fire pit and a hole for the rocks, cutting wood and assembling old blankets and tarps to cover the lodge. It was an all-day project that included lots of sweat and ingenuity and it brought us very close. When the lodge was completed late that afternoon we heated the rocks and entered, ready to sit on the damp earth, hot and naked together in a space that was very small and dark. This was the first time we had gotten so close, had really prayed and cried together. You learn very special things about people when you work and sweat with them.

Often there was discouragement in the beginning. Sometimes only one person would come, but we would sit and drum and be with one another in a ceremonial way, and engage in more intimate heartful talk, and persevere. Once when I was out of town no one came but Jana, who lived here on the same property with me. She had prepared cushions for each member and after drumming all alone, she smudged each cushion, speaking to each absent member as she did, thus keeping the energy of the circle alive. A teacher of mine once told me that the way to create an ongoing circle is to be there, and be there, and be there, until it takes hold and that was most certainly true in the case of this lodge.

Conflict came into our lodge the first year. Two of the original members had been studying with a neo-shaman who had studied with a tribe that believed the owl to be evil and dangerous. For several years owls had been coming into my field of consciousness powerfully, my house was full of owl presence, and it sat at the end of Owl Road. Because of this particular teacher's fears he cautioned the two women of the dangers of meeting with us, saying that we were surely practicing black magic. It became very quickly apparent that what he really feared was strong and independent women who really didn't need him or his authoritarian and fearful ways. One of the troubled women resigned immediately but the other remained with us for almost a year, going in and out of her apprehensions and suspicions.

Because the owl hunts by night, its flight is so silent, its call so eerie, and its hunting skills so exquisitely accurate, it has become to many a symbol of the dark and of death. For those who fear both it represents something to be avoided. It is also associated with the power of women and their involvement with the inner recesses of the soul and the unconscious realms. It is the Dark Goddess made manifest. This man's fear had brought these larger issues right into our circle and we decided to deal with them creatively and ceremonially.

We loved Rada's suggestion that we each make a black and a white mask to represent the light and the dark energies. We began to play very creatively with the masks. Once when the moon was dark we all dressed in black and wearing our black masks we walked deep into the canyon near my house and listened in silence to the night. Once when the moon was full we went to the beach at high noon dressed in white and wearing our white masks. We danced on the sand and spontaneously created a huge spiraling pattern that took us right to our center. Sometimes we would sit in circle wearing various combinations of black and white masks and speak to one another from the masks, learning all we could about those two energies, discovering the power and beauty in both the light and the dark.

We played and worked with these masks for a year. We creatively used ceremony to find power from the fear that had been brought into our circle. During this period the second woman who had been afraid of owlish power left for good, apparently unable to carry the tension this inner conflict brought into her life.

During this same period of time we went on a weekend camping trip together and used the time to create a shield. We used a large wooden hoop with a circle of leather lashed to it. Because of our work with the dark and light we painted one half of it white and one black. Margie drew an owl on one half and an eagle on the other, with wings overlapping into the opposite color. From this imagery we found our name, the Owl/ Eagle Lodge, the eagle representing the light, the bird that flies and hunts in the daytime, that has strong and far-reaching vision, and the owl, the one that flies by night and lives in the shadows. It represented much of what we had learned together, that the light always contains some darkness and the darkness always contains some light.

I had held a long-time enchantment with the dark and all its mysteries and yet this year had brought me a deeper understanding of the richness of those energies and made me even more eager to identify with their juicy and powerful womanliness.

We decided that it was time to declare a deeper level of commitment to our lodge and one another, so we agreed to each tie a feather that we had decorated in a unique manner to the shield to declare that commitment. We spontaneously created a wonderful ceremony as we each added our feather, declaring what we brought to the lodge, what we needed from it, and our level of commitment to it. It was a moving experience and took us to a new dimension together. It was clear to us that the way to inner power is through commitment. For us this worked to create a powerful lodge.

When a member leaves the circle we have a ceremony in which she removes her feather and ties a small shadow feather in its place so that her spirit energy remains present on the shield. When a new member comes we again recreate the tying-on ceremony and it re-reminds each of us of our promises to one another.

We have worked with many things in our lodge. An important issue is how so many powerful women can share power in graceful and honest ways. Some lodges deal with this by taking turns in leading meetings but we didn't do it that way. We chose a path that I believe to be more difficult and ultimately more rewarding. We decided to work with the power of silence, learning to sit together in absolute and utter silence, being with all the discomfort that can bring forth, until Spirit would come through one of us very clearly and with it direction and inspiration for our meeting. Sometimes nothing would come and it would be uncomfortable and boring and fairly discouraging.

This way seems much more empowering to me than passing the leadership from month to month. We have really said, "Let's don't have any leadership and see what happens. Let's allow Spirit to be the leader." We have had no real struggles around this issue and I find that to be most remarkable. There is something wonderfully revolutionary and empowering about this way and it really teaches how we can share power and allow for magic to enter. It seems to allow less room for ego and more for Spirit.

Sometimes we have created special ceremonies together. Usually when a member feels the need to have an important event ceremonialized she asks the group to create such a ritual. When I had my fiftieth birthday I asked the lodge sisters to design and lead a ceremony for me. Others have asked for special ceremonies when a baby was being born, they were getting married or divorced, or they were leaving the country to be gone a long while. Once we held a grieving ritual for a member who had a stillborn baby. Our rituals usually don't come from someone's need to lead one but rather in response to a sister's need to have something ritualized.

Occasionally a member will ask that we devote one or more meetings to a specific subject and will lead those meetings in exploring it. We spent several meetings with each telling our sexual stories to the circle and a couple of meetings talking about our ideas and feelings about death. Another circle was devoted to the issue of growing old, menopause, and claiming the power of age.

The women in this lodge are both very unique and quite ordinary. The group ranges in age from forty to the mid-fifties and comes from a wonderful variety of life experiences. Margie is the mother of two children and is an executive of a child care agency; Leah has a small daughter and is an acupuncturist; Alexandra is an artist, does desktop publishing, and is a grandmother; Amrita does computer-aided design for architects and

is a mother of a teen-aged son; Suzette has an adolescent son and a two-year-old and is a midwife; Jana, a single woman, is a speech therapist and makes rattles; KC is a psychotherapist and mother of a teenager; Margaret is a student who teaches flute and has three children, and Justine, mother of one grown son, is a radio producer. Ellen went on leave of absence when she had twins; Rada is living in Peru now, and Cynthus in Hawaii, and both have left a spirit-feather on our shield.

Some members of the Owl/Eagle Lodge preparing to begin a circle.

Leah was pregnant with her daughter when the lodge was a couple of years old so this little one heard the beat of the drum twice a month for nine months. Before Shayla was born we had a blessing way ceremony to welcome her into our lives and when she was tiny she would lie in her mother's arms during meetings. She doesn't come to meetings regularly but when she does come we all welcome her because her ceremonial manners are so fine. She sits in the circle, drums or rattles, and smudges the person next to her when it is her turn. She is always respectful of the circle and is never disruptive. She has been taught to honor it and as a result we all love it when she is present. Sometimes when I lead large ceremonial circles I invite her to do a specific part of the ritual because her ceremonial manners are so impeccable.

Conflict came again. Another member and I had a working arrangement outside the lodge and when it terminated it caused a conflict that affected the lodge. The other woman left the group and refused to come back to be part of a healing circle and to find a resolution. Many of the lodge members reached out to her individually but were not able to persuade her to return and be part of a healing circle, nor to come and remove her feather from the shield. Everyone was saddened by this, and we had to find ways of healing the circle without her presence.

We did learn something from this incident. When we take in new members now we ask them to commit to working through issues that might come up with other members, or with the entire circle, rather than leaving a hole in the circle that we have to work very hard to heal.

When the lodge was three years old we began to acknowledge the strength of our group and felt ready to begin to reach out to help other women find this way and the strength it brings. We began to network with the few other lodges we knew about and invited them to exchange power bundles with us as a way to connect the vision and spirit of the lodges.

A power bundle is a small pouch in which members place a small object that has strong symbolic meaning to them, such as a tiny rock found by a vision quester in the desert, a small crystal or gem stone, a few fragrant dried herbs, a wild animal's tooth, or a heart cut from red felt. We tie the bundles we receive from other lodges onto our shield, giving it an added magic and acknowledging our vision of thousands of lodges all over the world, finding their strength of purpose and creating social change through their connection within their lodges and with other lodges. It is a vision that combines the political and the spiritual, which seems to be one of our principal tasks in these times.

We also offer to help interested women create lodges and we sometimes journey to nearby towns to sit with groups of women the first time they meet to encourage them and tell them about what has and hasn't worked for us. When we first began to go together as a lodge to work with other groups of women we started getting a very clear sense of who we are as a lodge.

We decided to hold an open house, inviting women from our area to come and join us for an evening of drumming and ceremony. Eighty women came out to join with us in the pouring rain and it was an inspiring evening. We had placed our altar in the center and we sat around it in a small circle, drumming when the women arrived. They were smudged at the door and then took places sitting on the floor in a large circle around us, joining with us in the drumming and chanting. We told our lodge story to the group, how we have done things, what has worked and what hasn't. We had invited several other lodges to speak about their ways. Several new lodges began as a result of that evening.

Six months later we held another open house and this time one hundred and forty women came and this was even more exciting. This time two of our members led the group into an inner journey to find and talk to their "spirit grandmothers," to ask them if they should be in a lodge and if so, if they were to help in its creation, what it should be like, and other similar questions. This time there were many more women willing to make themselves available to be the ones who would focalize a lodge in the beginning period; others offered their homes as meeting places. The enthusiasm of the women had seemed to increase exponentially and our lodge had the sense that something we had been working toward for a long time was about to catch fire and burn brightly. We continue to hold these open houses twice a year.

We held another vision that we had shared with a local women's lodge when we were exchanging bundles with them. We wanted to co-host a weekend gathering of lodges and in the summer of 1988 the first annual gathering of Earth Lodges was held in northern California. Even though there had been a very enthusiastic response from a number of lodges, as the day approached we had only three, the two women's groups and a local men's lodge. We met for a weekend and decided to work on healing the wounds between women and men and continued to meet at regular intervals during the year to do this difficult and worthwhile work. Our dream of an annual gathering of lodges did come true and there is a story about it in the Community Stories section of this book.

MEN'S CIRCLES

There is a growing desire among men to redefine their masculine identity and an awareness that this is best accomplished in the company of brothers and wise elders. There is a focus on repairing the broken bond between fathers and sons and learning that the masculine includes being a nurturer, not just a provider. Men's circles provide a place to be real, to take risks of expression, and to acknowledge the beauty of a manhood deeply connected to the primal mysteries of the earth.

In these circles men learn to give and receive nurturance and approval from each other rather than relying solely on women for it. This alleviates a great strain in male-female relationships. As men learn to be nurturing fathers it mitigates this dependence at its root as the son finds solace and succor from his father.

A Men's Lodge

The night was soggy and fragrant with leaf mold and wet chaparral. Fifteen men sat on cushions or carpet squares around a wood fire on the ground in a suburban-rural backyard. The monthly meeting, at the dark

Bird Brother leading a circle for men in the Ukraine.

time of the moon, began with prayers to elemental deities, Earth, Air, Fire, and Water, spoken in a loud voice emphasized with the shaking of a rattle. Many of the men had drums.

A gnarled driftwood stick began circulating from one man to the next. As the stick came to him, each man took a turn leading the circle in a drummed rhythm, an improvised vocal chant, or some kind of body movement, sometimes while dancing energetically around the fire. Some men were visibly apprehensive as the stick approached, and with it the focused attention of the group. Others seemed confident or eager. As he held the stick each man looked for some authentic expression of voice or movement. Assurance came as he found it and the supporting echo of the fourteen other men swelled the rhythm into a sometimes rowdy crescendo, then relief and happiness as he passed the stick on to the next man.

One frightened man held the stick in tense silence for a few seconds, then said "I don't know what to say" in defeat, and tried to pass the stick. Other men in the circle looked at each other and repeated "I don't know what to say" several times until all were saying it in unison. A flash of compassion and awareness passed through the group at the uniquely male quality of pain that comes from being at a loss for words when we are supposed to be so expert, always ready. The voices became shouts. *"I don't know what to say"* became a raucous and hilarious chant. The frightened man, obviously moved and validated, joined in the chant with enthusiasm.

There was one teenager, brought by his father. He was given the job of tending the fire. Most were thirty-five to fifty years old, from a variety of professions, occupations, relationship status. One man was obviously gay-identified; with some others it was hard to tell. Two men were there for the first time, coming with a friend or associate, drawn to the idea of men meeting to really be themselves in the presence of other men, with no need to pose or compete.

The lodge had been started by a small group of friends. Two of them had attended a large men's gathering and the drumming and the deep male comradeship had made them hungry for more. They returned home with a strong commitment to call a men's circle and began to hold monthly meetings. News of the circle spread by word of mouth and soon the men realized that in meetings larger than eighteen or twenty there was a loss of intimacy, and it was difficult for each one to be heard. There was a further loss of intimacy when many of the group were new.

After several months of discussion about how to limit the size, and whether to be a closed or open group, a compromise was reached whereby anyone could bring a guest with the prior approval of the current month's leader. The result, while not as close as a committed closed circle, allowed both continuity and openness.

The stick began to go around a second time. This time the instructions were to speak from the heart about whatever one was dealing with emotionally in his life. For one it was the struggle to make a contracting business successful. For another it was the excitement of new love. Another was dealing with the grief of childhood innocence lost to the alcoholism and sexual abuse of an adult male relative. A man spoke with pride of being invited by his daughter to attend the birthing of his first grandchild.

At the end of this second go-around, the stick was placed on a small altar and the time was open for announcements, plans, proposals. Some of the men were planning an art therapy workshop. Others were involved in a campaign to stop the use of herbicides along county highways. Someone needed to be chosen to represent the group in the planning of an upcoming council of women's and men's lodges. The teenager was thanked enthusiastically for his presence and his attention to the fire.

The men all stood, and the gnarled stick was passed from hand to hand around the circle. Whoever wanted could take the stick and hold it until the next new moon, and thereby take responsibility for the time, place, and plan of the next meeting. Some, ready for the meeting to end, passed the stick quickly. Some lingered with it, as if they would like to take it but had too many other responsibilities. At last a man took the stick with conviction, raised it over his head, and the others cheered.

The evening's holder of the stick made a short prayer to the elemental deities, thanking each one for the gifts of the meeting, and the circle was ended. The men began socializing, with lots of hugging, joking, and physical contact, and gradually dispersed from the glow of the fire in ones and twos into the damp darkness.

It had been an ordinary new moon meeting, with no special agenda other than the temporary leader's hope to emphasize the body and the feelings rather than mental discourse, an emphasis many men find as thrilling as it is difficult.

In the short three years since the circle formed the men had many nonordinary meetings. One was a fathers and sons night, where all the men were encouraged to bring their father and/or son with them to the meeting. At another one daughters were honored. There was a special meeting to initiate one fellow who had big new family responsibilities into the role of father/provider. At one meeting each man brought a photograph of himself as a child and told about learning to ride his first bicycle. At another one the men responded to a challenge to deal with issues of incest and sexual abuse.

They did sweat lodges and Sufi dances, Tibetan Buddhist chant cycles and Neo-pagan charm-work. They prayed and sang. They played ball. They arranged rocks and crystals into a garage-sized mandala. Most of all they designed their own ritual and ceremony or modified familiar ones to suit the people and the occasion, combining fragments of old traditions with impromptu imagination and intuition, trying to reconnect to some original source of earth and belly wisdom they recognized in each other and in the circle.

A Drumming Story

Drumming is about keeping the issue of liberation alive, so we can speak to each other in a real language. There has to be a great and driving urge to communicate before people take the time to find out what exists between them. Drumming is a community-building action and is a very precise and intricate art form.

Getting a cohesive drumming circle going requires a commitment that is very deep because it is in the realm of Spirit. As I write these words I feel the presence of Mohammed, a favorite drumming buddy of mine. He is from Morocco and is a traditional musician of that culture. I feel the spirit presence of Rick, a master drummer on many different drums, who helped me call in the spirit of my son.

Before every drumming session I like to take a moment to internally remember and connect with all who have drummed before me. This is the way that I have found to worship the Ancestors. Drumming is a spirit-opening act. Teachings will come flooding in, and don't think you have to do it one way or another. Drumming should not be confined; anything percussive that anybody does upon any surface or hollow, on the side of an oil drum, or telephone pole, is drumming. Or with the feet. Many of the first drums were big enough to dance on and the drumming was done with the feet. A drummer is anyone who wants to drum who is willing to listen to the inner pulse of the earth.

The purpose of the drum is to make an accessible way for people to get harmonized and magnetized and vibrated by a common, from the heart-pulse-beat. The healing potential of the drum is awesome.

One time Mohammed and I were walking in the early morning at a big festival where there were to be twenty to thirty thousand people. We stopped walking and were lounging and talking on a bench in the warm summer sun. We had our drums with us and started playing. There were already hundreds of people around, vendors setting up their stalls, craftspeople, folks out on walks before the festivities of the day began.

A "retarded" boy came and sat between us and started putting his head on our drums, hugging us and making sounds. It made me a little nervous but not Mohammed. I looked at the parents and they were watching their child with awe. It seemed as if it was the first time he had responded like that in a long time to anything. I got over my paranoia and we just let that boy make all the funny sounds and body contortions he wanted to. Whatever he needed to feel was all right and the whole time his parents were beaming us their love-affirmations.

When I play drums with Mohammed it is always special because something in his radiance reminds me to pray for peace and it feels like the dialogue we have with our instruments sends out a healing ray between our peoples. By playing and listening to each other, by loving each other as brothers while we celebrate the holiness of the circle of life, we set into motion some little bit of mending.

POLITICAL CIRCLES

By gathering in small cohesive circles we establish a core of living energy that can be joined with other circles. These small and powerful circles, connected together, form a global community. The intimate, cohesive circle is the generating point of the global network.

The only way to save the environment is for it to become part of our identity. If we allow our local environment, our neighborhood, to be defiled, then the whole world will be defiled. If we are united in our search for balance and harmony, then we must do something about the destruction, even if it is only to be a conscious witness.

Our work is to bring balance and harmony, both inside and outside. This is a simultaneous process. Though we have made advances on the spiritual path by going inside there is also a time, if that inner learning is to become real, that it must be put into practice. Meditation and personal enlightenment alone do not fulfill the spiritual quest. Those approaches to union were effective at a particular time for a particular place but it is now time to make acts of power in the world. This is why the image of the spiritual warrior is so potent.

The work of the spiritual warrior is to bring balance and harmony. We all must risk safety and the security of the known in favor of decisions that speak on behalf of the earth. It is time for acts of courage that honor life. The principal motivation for us in writing this book is to inspire people to form circles that protect and defend the earth and all her children. Natural systems are deteriorating right before our eyes. The air is getting so polluted that the sunlight is becoming dangerous. There is a hole in the ozone layer and the oceans are dying. We live in the midst of the most serious ecological crisis that has ever existed on this planet and if we do not make it part of our spiritual practice to restore balance there will be nothing left but ashes.

We live in a violent world. Nation against nation, race against race, religion against religion, enemies projected outward, more than half the gross national product expended toward war. Meanwhile the environment dies. The energy expended outward to fight off the enemy is directly proportional to the defilement of the environment.

When we circle we hear the beauty of the earth's song and also the pain and desperation. The circle empowers us to feel the totality of our being and to utilize its form to unite the spiritual with the political. This is something that none of us knows much about but we are in the process of finding ways to make this union powerful and effective.

On the Beach

The sun is touching the water and the just-full moon is rising from the east. The circle has been smudged and a song is being composed. The fire is not needed for warmth anymore. The beach is deserted, except for the circlers, who will stay all night. A child cries and is suckled. The moon passes overhead and slowly descends into the ocean, spreading its golden

Families hold hands in prayer at the beach.

light across the mind-fields of the Goddess. The songs continue through-out the night and the drum never stops, determined, sad, angry. There might be an oil-drilling rig built here soon and the beach will no longer be a sanctuary. It hasn't happened yet and there is a possibility that it won't, but the circlers know that to stop the destruction will require a miracle. They pray and dance and sing for that miracle. Some have vowed, during the long night, to actively stop the building of the drilling rigs. Some are willing to risk their lives. They especially will need a miracle.

In the Woods

A circle has formed in an area where an old-growth forest is to be clear-cut. The lumber company owns the land and thinks it has the right to harvest its crop. The circle thinks that the trees have a right to exist and that this particular grove should be saved so that people may know what it is like to feel thousand-year-old spirits. The circlers know they have received valuable teachings from these trees. They feel in their hearts that they want their children and grandchildren also to have access to these teachings.

The date is set when the logging operation is to begin. That morning the circle holds a council as the loggers arrive for work. The people in the circle know that the workers are not their enemies and there is no hostility

A small group of people drumming and dancing in front of the Department of Forestry to protest the clear-cutting of old-growth trees.

toward them, though some of the loggers regard the circlers with fear and suspicion.

The circlers rise and walk into the sacred grove, each standing before a tree, placing shells and feathers at its base. As they do this they tell the trees they want them to live.

In this instance the circlers were not able to save the sacred grove but they did witness and in witnessing they shared a powerful bond, which gave them the strength and courage to keep the faith. Circling gave them the initiative to defend the place and provided them support for acts of earth protection. Moving in circle harmonized them with the natural energies and expressions of the earth and increased their capacity to hear the earth speak.

Dancing for the Trees

Once a month a group of people who call their group The Sacred Grove meets at noon in front of the Department of Forestry in a town in northern

California. The Department has a policy of routinely approving the clear-cutting of the beautiful giant redwood trees in that area. There are only four percent of the old-growth redwood groves left in the state. The situation is serious and is being addressed by environmentalists in the courts. This group was organized to approach the problem in a different way, wishing instead to appeal to the spirit and the heart of these bureaucrats.

After the group has been smudged this small band of people dances in front of the Forest Service office for two hours in a slow, repetitive step, circling around a drummer who sits in the center of the circle. Sometimes someone in the circle will begin a spontaneous song, or a call and response with the other dancers. Many of them shake rattles or drum as they dance. Some wear black armbands to show their mourning for the trees and all the birds and other wildlife who make their homes in the forest and are being destroyed mindlessly. When the dance ends the group holds hands and prayers are offered.

This same group of people formed the core of a large circle ceremony held in the courthouse square. It was dedicated to the owls who live in the redwood groves, and whose lives are being destroyed. It was a spiritual plea to the consciousness of those who can decide the fate of the forests.

Circle to Reclaim Sacredness and Safety

A woman was raped on a Sunday morning while running on a walking path in a small town. The circle was called on the following Sunday morning by a local peace group. About seventy-five women and men gathered on the same path and walked in silence along it, following two women playing a heartbeat rhythm on their drums, all mindful of the atrocity perpetrated here and all the many others who are raped and abused.

When the group arrived at the site they formed a circle and after the circle was cast various people read poems and statements and led a few songs. A small rock carved as a goddess was passed to each person in the circle and they were asked to speak their feelings, prayers, and commitments and to place these into the goddess-rock as they held it in turn. A woman and man then buried the goddess along the pathway, reclaiming the area as sacred ground and asking for protection for all those who pass there. Everyone left the circle committed to finding ways to end violence against women.

Service Circle

There is a service circle that meets once a month in our area to define and share issues of environmental concerns and to give support to one another

A circle formed in response to a rape. The circle gathered at the site to reclaim the ground there as sacred and to help heal the wounds caused by violence toward women.

in finding solutions that include Spirit. The circle always begins with drumming, smudging, and calling in the elemental spirits. The talking stick is passed and members of the circle speak about their concerns and ask for any support they need for projects or ecological groups they are associated with. It can be a safe place for people to express their fears and their despair about the plight of the world and the group will be witness to it, knowing that when despair comes up for the others they will also have ears willing to hear.

Once, in response to a member's concern about litter on nearby beaches, the group planned a picnic outing to the ocean to clean up the area together. They have planted trees and written letters to representatives and senators. At each meeting they take some kind of action rather than just talk about acting. Their motto is "Let's Walk Our Talk."

Their purpose is to encourage one another in their efforts to make small but meaningful changes in the world. They are in the process of networking with other service circles in other areas and have a newsletter to help make that happen. The group is family-oriented and the children

A small goddess is ceremonially buried at the rape site by a woman and man.

are encouraged to be part of the projects, as a way of modeling concerned action for them.

The group has made a shield that they will take to rallies and political events. It is circular and is divided into twelve wedges and various members have painted symbols in the wedges that represent different concerns the group has, such as whales and dolphins, the rain forest and the redwoods, the ozone, the waters, and the animal kingdom.

COMMUNITY CIRCLES

Community circles provide an opportunity to gather with people that we may not know but with whom we share a common heart-path. They give us a broader sense of neighborhood and sometimes an opportunity to experience ourselves as part of a global family.

In this section we have included stories that encompass a variety of community events, and in one of the stories the community includes the nonhuman members of the global family. In another the community includes the sun and the moon.

Sedonia leading a large ceremonial circle in the Ukraine as part of an exchange program of healers.

City Ceremony

Powerful ceremonial events can take place in concert halls and auditoriums. One of the most important public ceremonies I, Joshua, have ever attended was a concert with Gabrielle Roth, an urban shaman, and Fantuzzi, the wizard of New Age rock. It was held at the Kabuki Theater in San Francisco's Japantown. Fantuzzi played first and got everyone moving and then Gabrielle and her band came on. With her poetic invoking and dancing she brought the whole group into unity and something extraordinary happened. The audience was so ready and in-tune that the line between performer and audience was crossed. The stage area became part of the dance, as people circled around the auditorium they began to dance across it.

The transformation of the audience into a pulsating, tribal entity happened so smoothly and well it was as if it had been choreographed and rehearsed. The dancing was superb, the music was excellent, and everyone felt a great sense of oneness. The event showed me what a powerful force shamanic rock is and how hungry the urban community is for ceremony.

Four Seasonal Circles

The solstices and equinoxes mark the changing seasons and remind us of the life cycle. The modern world seems to see life as a series of events, progressing in a linear way from beginning to end, from birth to death, and then it's all over. This is a difficult position to maintain and has required a great deal of effort, because life is really much more about cycles; what dies is reborn, and then dies and is reborn again.

Seasons come and go, things change, renew and decay, nothing stays the same, yet all will return in its time. Honoring and celebrating the turning of the wheel of the year reminds us of the ways the polarities inside of us move and change. At times the days are short, then they become longer, then shorter again, at times the days and the nights are equal in length and power; all is change, all is movement.

THE SPRING EQUINOX

The spring equinox marks the time when the long winter nights have become shorter and the light that was promised in the winter begins to overcome the cold and darkness. The days are getting longer, the grasses green and the first flowers are beginning to blossom.

A circle of twelve women and men gathers on a sunny slope of land that opens onto the eastern horizon. They have decided to meet at dawn to honor the first rays of the sun on this day, March 21. They sit on blankets on the damp grass in silence until the sun begins to peep over the distant hill, then they all begin to chant a greeting.

Everyone has brought a seed and someone places a large pot of soil in the center. People in turn plant their seeds saying what of themselves they are seeding, and as they pour water on it they say how they will be nourishing this part. All in the circle chant "We bless this new beginning" as the seeds are planted.

Each has brought a flower, saying what in them is blossoming at this time, as they place it in the center. After each speaks the others in the circle chant "We welcome this flower into our circle."

One person has brought freshly made bread and another fresh juice, another fruit, and all this is shared in a way that honors these foods and one another. There is laughter and hopefulness in this circle and a strong sense of renewal.

THE SUMMER SOLSTICE

The summer solstice, which comes on June 21, marks the time when the sun is at its apex. This is the longest day of the year, the rays of the sun are strong and hot, and the energy is light and fun-filled. The group of more than thirty women and men has met at a protected and isolated cove at the ocean, just before noon.

The drums are playing as people arrive, some joining in with their drums or rattles, some chanting and dancing. There are children in and out of the circle, excited by the music and the ocean.

The music stops and there is only the sound of the waves breaking on the shore, the wind blowing lightly and cooling the day. The directions and the elements are called to enter and protect this circle, this time with song and dance. Everyone sits on the sand, a staff is passed, and each person speaks of the part of her- or himself that is in full bloom, bursting with life and enthusiasm. One person tells of a new work project that can bring relief to the whales, another of a new relationship that seems to be the answer to a long-held prayer, one woman who will be giving birth in a couple of months shows her belly so full of life, another who has been working on a book for a long time has just completed the manuscript, a small child smiles and shows two new teeth. Everyone in the circle is delighted to be witness to these blossomings.

Everyone holds hands and there are some songs and prayers and then the entire circle moves toward the ocean singing:

Born of water, cleansing, powerful, healing, changing, I am

Everyone in the group, still in a large circle, moves into the cold water, still singing and holding hands. The hands all rise to the sky, there are loud whoops and yells and lots of laughter and splashing. When everyone has reassembled on the sand the circle is made again, the directions thanked, and there is a blessing for the food that everyone has brought to share.

THE AUTUMN EQUINOX

The days and nights are equal in length once again. The harvest is in and it is time to prepare for the dark, cold nights that will be growing longer. It is time to move inward and to look deep inside.

The group has gathered in a large teepee. It is the evening of September 21 and because it is cool outside, there is a fire crackling in the fire pit in the center. The sacred circle is established with drumming, smudging, and invoking. Everyone has been asked to bring something to place on the altar that represents some part of themselves that is no longer needed, that is ready to die.

As the staff passes each person places her or his object on the altar that is to the west of the fire circle. One places a nail to represent long-held anger for his father, one a broken nutshell to represent the protective armor she has worn for so long, another woman places a photo of the lover who no longer wants her, a man places a package of cigarettes that he says he is finished with forever. To place these things on the altar is to say "these things once served me in some way, and I honor them for that, but now I am ready to let them go, and I ask each of you to be witness to this commitment."

The group sings a song:

Sacred Earth Mother come to me, make my life sacred, fill me with beauty

Now one of the men asks the people to make themselves comfortable as he begins to lead them through an inner meditation/journey into the deep to find the answers to some questions. "What am I harvesting of myself at this time? What in me is ready to die?" When the meditation is over the staff passes and each person tells the answers she or he found to these questions in the guided meditation.

Next someone places a freshly baked loaf of bread on the table, and some grape juice, which are passed in the circle and each person feeds the person on his or her left, expressing the abundance of the harvest season.

Prayers are said, the directions thanked, and the circle closes.

THE WINTER SOLSTICE

This is a deeply mystical time for many. It is the longest night of the year, all have gone deep inside and faced the long dark night of the soul, and now await the return of the sun.

This circle is held in a large room. It is late in the evening of December 21 and the room is dark. Everyone is smudged at the door as they arrive and are given a small, unlit votive candle. When the drumming and chanting end and the directions are called, the group is guided on a meditation to find the Magical Spirit Child within. When the meditation is ended, one by one people in the circle come forward, holding their candles. They tell of this child and light a candle in its honor as they place it on the altar. As they do this they make a spoken commitment to the child within and to all the children. This is a large circle and the effect of having so many candles, lit one by one and placed on the altar, is breathtaking. It helps everyone to see what beauty is possible when each person brings forth his or her spirit child. Everyone sings:

This little light of mine
I'm gonna let it shine
This little light of mine
I'm gonna let it shine
This little light of mine
I'm gonna let it shine
Let it shine, let it shine, let it shine

A tray is passed and on it are small squares (2″ × 2″) of red cotton fabric, small pieces of green yarn or ribbon, a pouch of tobacco, a small bowl of cornmeal, and little bunches of various herbs, and dried flowers. Everyone in the circle takes a piece of fabric, yarn, and any herbs they want to use for making small bundles. Silent prayers are given as the bundles are made. A very long piece of red yarn is passed around the circle and everyone ties their prayer bundle on it, about six inches apart.

The youngest person in the circle, a four-year-old girl, with a little help from her mother, slowly wraps the yarn with the bundles around a small tree on the altar as the group sings:

> We are weaving our magic
> We are weaving our power
> We are weaving our love

When this is done someone volunteers to take the tree wrapped with the bundles home, promising to plant it in a special place where it will receive care and nurturing. This is to encourage all the prayers that were placed on it.

The group stands and holds hands and, slowly moving to the left, a dance begins, drummers in each direction, dancers shuffling to the left in a simple left-foot-step, right-foot-follow, one-two one-two beat, as everyone sings:

> We are creating a circle of light, AH OM
> We are creating a family of light, AH OM
> We are creating a nation of light, AH OM
> We are uniting with a universal light, AH OM, AH OM

When the dance is ended everyone is given the opportunity to speak prayers, the directions are thanked, and the circle ended.

Everyone leaves this circle with a beautiful and inspiring memory of the solstice tree, heavy laden with prayers, standing in the midst of all the Spirit candles.

Gathering of the Waters Ceremony

A group of people who meet once a year for a large ceremonial gathering were each asked to bring a small container of water from a body of water that was special to them. Because these people came from all parts of the country the waters were from two oceans thousands of miles apart, from a number of different lakes and rivers, and from the gulf to the south. Someone had brought water from the Ganges River in India. One who had lived through a very difficult year brought a vial of her own tears and another woman who was struggling to love her body brought her menstrual blood.

This group of thirty people made a circle around a recently dug hole in the earth that had been lovingly decorated with wreaths and flowers, and each in turn poured the liquid they had carried into the hole, telling the story of the water and giving blessings as they poured. Then the large

Sun Dance pole that Elizabeth Cogburn's dancers dance around for three long days and nights was placed in the hole and all were ready to begin the dance.

A variation of this circle can be done any time people gather from various places to do ceremony together.

Tree-Planting Ceremony

A local high school planned to plant three trees for Earth Day on the campus and wanted to do it in a ceremonial way. The ceremony was held in the afternoon after school so that only those who were really interested would come. The group met in a circle around the area that had been prepared for the trees. Some had brought their drums and they began to play. The ground, the unplanted trees, and the people were smudged with sage and the powers of the elements were called to witness the ceremony.

One of the people responsible for the ceremony spoke of the trees, how they would serve the students, creating shade and beauty, and how in turn they would need water and appreciation from them. All the nonhuman creatures that would make their homes near or in these trees were invited to their new homes. The students were asked to remember that they could find nurture and solace from these trees and that in many ways they were much alike. Both had deep roots that reach into the earth, the tree's roots visible, the humans' roots not so clearly seen. Both the trees and the humans stand tall and reach heavenward, supported by the earth, warmed and nourished by the sun, washed and fed by the rains.

The trees were then placed in the holes that had been prepared for them and some students who had brought small containers of water poured them on the trees. Others put handfuls of dirt into the hole. Some spoke blessings for the trees, some were silent. Some of the students stayed to play the drums a little longer, seeming to want to linger with these newfound friends.

Council of All Beings

The nonhuman forms of life have few ways to be heard since most of us have forgotten how to listen to them. It is rare that their needs and wishes are understood or considered. They are disappearing at alarming rates. One hundred species a day are becoming extinct because we have forgotten to listen, forgotten that they are all at least as important as we are in the hoop of life. The Council of All Beings is a way that humans can begin to be sensitive to the voices of these wordless ones and learn to speak their needs for them in human councils. The Council of All Beings was

A circle of masks at a Ceremonial Long Dance. *Photo: Elizabeth Cogburn*

developed by Joanna Macy and John Seed, and the following ceremonial adaptation was inspired by their work.

A group of forty women and men came together in the activity room of a local university. The sacred circle was called in with smudging and invoking and a brief explanation of the intent was spoken by the woman who was to lead the circle. Round white paper plates, paints, crayons, glue, scissors, and small odds and ends such as raffia, feathers, pipe cleaners, and small sticks were placed in the center of the circle.

After a period of drumming the group was led through a guided meditation to find the life form they each were to represent. They were given twenty minutes to assemble a mask from the supplies in the center that would resemble the being that had called to them. The mask was to help them move from their own persona into the spirit of this other life form.

After the supplies were removed the group was asked to spend some time making the movements and sounds of those they represent, while wearing their masks.

With everyone sitting in a circle on the floor, the staff was passed and each person spoke a message from his or her mask. "I am the ocean, wild and free," "I am the wolf, keeper of the tribes," "I am the mountain lion, graceful and strong," "I am the aspen tree and I sing in the wind," "I am the vulture and I transform death into life." All are qualities that the nonhumans carry and that we humans can learn about through observing them.

After each had spoken the group divided into two parts and one group moved into the center of the circle facing outward. They removed their masks because now they were to represent the humans. The group in the outer circle, still wearing their masks, began to speak, telling the humans their distress and the danger that they face. "I am the fresh river streams and I am choking from your waste," "I am the great grizzly bear and you kill me for sport," "I am the wolf and I want to keep my tribe strong but you have poisoned and shot so many of my kin," "I am the spotted owl and you are destroying my forest home," "I am the wild poppy and you are bulldozing my fields to make more tract houses," "You are cruel," "You are greedy," "You have forgotten the sacred ways," "You must stop what you are doing and remember we are all related."

The two groups exchanged places and the new group in the outer circle, wearing their masks, spoke their pain and suffering to the humans in the center. Now everyone moved into the larger circle and there were songs and prayers and the circle closed.

This circle is disturbing to be part of but each person leaves better understanding the situation of the other species and more determined and committed to taking care of the life on this earth.

Annual Gathering of Earth Lodges

Once a year, in midsummer, there is a weekend gathering of women's and men's lodges in northern California. Groups come from all over the state to meet with each other, to learn of one another's ways, to get inspiration, to council on real issues, and to have fun.

It is held on a beautiful piece of land that is owned by a community of people who feed the group delicious food that is grown in their organic garden. Everyone brings tents or sleeps under the trees and the meetings are held in a beautiful meadow with a splendid view of the ocean.

There is a large circle the first morning in which each lodge is given time to introduce themselves and tell or demonstrate something about the flavor and purpose of their circle. There are groups just for women, or for men, and groups that are mixed. Some are inspired by European paganism and others by native ways; most are a blend of many ways.

Later the larger group breaks into small groups to discuss specific issues. The first year the topic was "Healing between women and men through telling the truth to one another." The second year the issue was, "What is our responsibility to one another as brothers and sisters?"; another year the issue was "How do we mix Spirit and politics?"

In the evenings there are circles for storytelling and singing, and sometimes ceremonial circles to take everyone to deep places together. The final morning the large circle usually has elements of dance and song and celebration, everyone feeling delighted to have spent time with so many people on the healing path together.

At the first gathering a bundle was made by the group, which was to be held and cared for by someone during the year, each time being brought back to the council gathering. This was a way to keep the energy strong and growing.

Each year there are three or four dance chiefs, people whose job it is to design and choreograph all the events, assign various tasks to different people, and be responsible that things run smoothly and easily. These dance chiefs are from different lodges and volunteer for the job. Each year conflicts arise and as time passes we are learning better ways to deal with them.

We have a vision of such councils happening all over, all networked together, sharing ideas and ways and creating a strong network for social change.

Harmonic Convergence

The Harmonic Convergence was prototypic of the power of circling. What began as the insightful research of one man, Dr. Jose Arguelles, became the largest simultaneously coordinated act of prayer, meditation, and ceremony ever to take place at sacred sites throughout the world. The philosophical basis for the convergence was complex, though its general thesis is quite simple: It is time to acknowledge the earth as our sacred altar.

The focal point of the Convergence was August 16 and 17, 1987, corresponding to the ancient prophecy of Mexico and Central America, which pinpoints the return of Quetzalcoatl, Lord of the Dawn. Another ancient prophecy comes from the Lakota Sioux, stating that the sacred pipe which White Buffalo Woman brought to the people was to be brought out once again to help the people remember that all things are sacred. This prophecy purportedly came true on the summer solstice of 1987.

The success of the Harmonic Convergence depended on community grassroots efforts that drew upon celebratory endeavors and collective artistic outpourings of all kinds. Concerts, ritual, dance and theater events, and outdoor circles of every sort created a global fair woven together by the media into a unique celebration whose goal was to raise the human spirit through a single collective experience.

These days were celebrated all over the world. In North America some of the main gathering sites were Mount Shasta and Mount Tamalpais in California, and Chaco Canyon in New Mexico. Other gatherings happened at Stonehenge, Machu Picchu, the pyramids in Egypt, Australia, Hawaii, Mexico City, and other places scattered all over the globe as hundreds of thousands of people gathered in circles.

We decided to coordinate one of the convergence gatherings on Mount Tamalpais, a mountain that overlooks the entire Bay Area in Marin County. We began by printing and distributing a simple flyer announcing our intention to call a gathering. We held a series of circles, each attended by approximately thirty people, to discuss our plans and to sit in council to share our feelings about the Convergence.

Unknown to us we were networked into several umbrella organizations that distributed information about us all over the country. Several weeks before the event we began to receive hundreds of calls from people all over the state, and a few from out-of-state, asking for information and whether they could join us. We said yes to everyone, that it was an open circle. We subsequently learned that there were going to be three other circles on the mountain, two of which were limited in the number of people allowed to participate. One large event was to be held in the amphitheater and we were asked to lead a ceremony in it on the final day.

The Harmonic Convergence struck a chord and provided people with a living myth of which they could be a part. People from all walks of life were expressing their need for a new cycle of creation to begin. It was astounding. The phone would ring and a few minutes later it would ring again. People from here, people from there, all wanting to be part of this thing called the Harmonic Convergence. The anvil of time had perfectly formed a need and now it was to be filled. We began to hear stories of what the Convergence meant to others.

We wanted to keep our focus on the earth and really hear the earth speaking. We had heard enough to know that she had something to say that was very important to human beings everywhere. We were feeling from the earth that we had been dependent on her for so long, without knowing or appreciating her, and now it was time for us to take care of her.

Our challenge was to keep the focus and be ready for the unknown. Even when you know how many people are going to come to a circle it is best to go to the place and feel it out. When you don't know how many people are going to come it is imperative. So we explored the mountain and got a renewed feeling for the land so that we would know how to form the circle. The land was our guide and we kept open and prayed.

For four days Bird and I, Sedonia, walked with a small group around the base of the mountain, stopping each night at one of the directions, making our prayers and calling in Spirit. We would sleep there and the next day walk on to the next direction. In this way we were honoring the mountain and notifying it of our intentions. During these days we came to know the mountain in ways that we hadn't before. We saw an amazing variety of beautiful terrain, tall redwood circles, manzanita groves that looked like spider webs, creeks and waterfalls, damp forests of fern, meadows that looked like brown velvet. We ate from wild apple trees, blackberry and huckleberry bushes, miners lettuce. We saw deer and squirrels and raccoons and many birds. We bathed in icy cold pools of water. We walked through poison oak and got scratched by thorns and bitten by mosquitos and climbed when we were too tired to even walk. By the time of the Saturday night ritual we felt we had earned the right to lead ceremony on the mountain.

At four o'clock on Sunday morning we rang bells to awaken everyone and we gathered for an hour-long peace meditation. People all over the earth were meditating at that time and we all felt very supported by that global circle.

There were several thousand people on the mountain and several hundred of them were with us. We came from all walks of life, most of us had never met before, and yet we had agreed to come together for two days and nights of ceremony to express our concerns for the earth and our commitment to personal and global transformation.

During those two days and nights we met in many different circles. Twice we made sacred fires. The first time we each offered some token that symbolized an outmoded part of ourselves we were ready to relinquish to make way for the new days to come. The second fire was made the next morning and in it we placed things to represent our pledge to the future and to peace. Another time we came together in a large circle in a meadow on the mountain to dance in a clockwise circle around drummers standing in each of the directions. Earlier in the afternoon we had all gone off alone to spend several hours meditating and listening to the earth and during the dance each person moved into the center of the circle to speak, sing, or dance the message they had received.

We ended at noon the final day by walking counterclockwise on a pathway near the summit, offering prayers of gratitude to each direction, drumming and singing as we walked. We chose to walk counterclockwise in order to send our prayers outward and into the world. Our original four-day walk had been in a clockwise direction in order to concentrate our intention and our energies so that our ceremonies would be strong and vital.

The most significant thing about the Convergence was the way it formed and where it was held. It is a good example of a public ceremonial, open to all and free of charge. On Sunday morning there were over four thousand people on the mountain, most in small clusters. Due to the geography there was no central circle, which in some respects was too bad because many people came to the mountain to be part of a community but instead were left to discover their own inner resources. However the power of thousands of people praying on a mountain, connected to thousands of other circles all over the earth, is something that will stay with us for a long time. It was very inspiring that so many people could circle together to express a vision of peace and harmony.

EIGHT

MENDING THE SACRED HOOP

Only within burns the fire I kindle.
My heart the altar.
My heart the altar.
POEM OF A BUDDHIST NUN

The Hopi Indians, known as the People of Peace, say that the Sacred Hoop represents the unbroken observance of the laws of harmony and balance with all things. Everything has a place in the hoop; insects, lichen, whales, redwood trees, grizzly bears, vultures, humans. Each is an expression of Spirit, full and complete in itself, yet interdependent on the whole. Human beings left their place within the hoop when they began to think they were separate and superior and that all other life forms had been given to them to use as they pleased. Some humans stepped even further out and began to use other humans to serve their greed and lust.

RECLAIMING THE SOUL

Ancient stories from many traditions have prophesied a time when the balance would be restored, when people from all parts of the world would come together in peace, bringing wisdom, love, and compassion. The time to restore the Sacred Hoop is now if we are to survive with dignity.

To restore the balance we need to envision ourselves as part of the whole rather than holding to a narrow identification of self. The three divisions that have most factionalised us, race, class, and gender, all have to be worked through as part of the process of finding our way back into the hoop. Human factionalism diverts our attention away from attending to the real survival issues we are faced with right now. Yet it also seems that before people are able to step back into oneness they have to feel a sense of worth and pride in themselves. This phase of identification is often very important but it needs to be understood as one step toward the many we need to bring us into a greater unification.

The work we are all faced with is that of recovering our soul-force, Ahimsa, that particular strength that compels us to right thought, work, and action. Each time we are abused, or abuse, there is a diminishing of this soul-force within ourselves. Every time we collude and don't speak up when we see injustice, every time we make choices that don't honor or serve life, we suffer a degree of soul loss.

The process of reclaiming soul-force is one of finding our way back into our belly-wisdom where we are both wise and innocent, and has to be worked on every day. Part of this reclaiming is rediscovering the pleasures that were ours while we still had our innocence. Dancing, singing, telling our magical story, and honoring and enjoying the silence are all parts of the practice of reclaiming.

As we begin to do these things and find pleasure and joy within ourselves we become more self-sufficient and are drawn toward a life of simplicity, based on earth-centered values rather than endless consumption. When we find our own self-worth we no longer need to measure ourselves by society's criteria. This involves the choices we make every day about how we earn and spend our money, what foods we choose, whether we compost and recycle, whether we are thoughtful about our use of electricity and gasoline, whether we are kind and open with our neighbors. This is a matter of making ethical choices, one-day-at-a-time decisions, which are good for our personal welfare and in turn benefit our family, community, and the earth. It can be thought of as a *sadhana*, or daily spiritual practice, for ecological, political, and communal awareness. It is through making good small choices that we develop the integrity to make larger political/spiritual ones.

It is wonderful to discover that what is really good for us is also really good for the earth and that every time we make a life-affirming choice it both strengthens and sensitizes us. This has the effect of balancing the polarities, the male and female energies, within ourselves.

When we become part of a circling community that allows us to do re-souling work we can find our way back into knowing who we really are. It is from this knowing, deep in our belly, that we develop Ahimsa. It is the development and unfolding of Self, within the context of community, that generates the soul-force which will bring us back into the Sacred Hoop.

One of the spiritual challenges that we each face is to create within ourselves a circle that is very large and inclusive. This begins with questioning ourselves about who and what we feel kinship with, who and what is in our spirit-circle. Then we need to consider who and what we feel alienated from, different than, and how we exclude them from our circle.

Attendant to the development of soul-force is compassion. To learn compassion we need to develop the muscles of our heart so that we are capable of allowing everyone to dance in it. A compassionate being is one whose heart is generous and wise enough to understand that the circle is not complete unless all things have a place within it.

REWEAVING THE STORY

We live in a time when it is necessary to weave a new story together. For centuries many have believed the old story about separateness; nation against nation; human against nature; that some people deserve more than others. We have endlessly dramatized and rationalized the battle between the sexes. We have believed that our children were our property, that might made right, that there was not enough to go around. These are part of an obsolete paradigm.

Each of us has a personal obsolete paradigm that says we are not worthwhile just as we are, that we need more possessions to be content, that it is someone else's fault that we haven't gotten where we wanted to go, that our personal behavior does not affect the whole, that we are powerless to change the world and save the earth.

Through finding a circling community, developing soul-force and a spirit that encompasses the great circle, we collectively weave a new story that honors the four great mysteries a myth that inspires and encourages us. As we weave this story let us tell it as if it is already accomplished, all the while doing whatever we need to do to make it so.

We may, if we keep to the circling process, be able to provide the living fuel for what will be known as one of the most profound revolutions of all time. Of course this will depend entirely upon whether we have the courage and physical stamina to go about our daily, necessary survival tasks without taking more than we give and if we all, within our circles, support one another in this life-work.

To build a renewable, sustainable culture is to find our way back into the Sacred Hoop and it requires that we develop the shamanic power to call back all the pieces of the great dance through dreams and vision, through songs and the ceremonial arts. Each of us holds a thread in this tapestry that we are weaving which is vital, numinous, and essential. May we each hold our thread with strong intention, integrity, fierceness, and beauty.

Meditation

We invite you to come with us for a moment into sacred time and space, into a way of seeing that is broad and spacious. We ask you to see this day, from the time you arose this morning until you sleep this evening, as one ceremony, divided into small and familiar rituals, your heart as the altar. You, part of the cycles of light and darkness.

Now begin to see your life, from the moment of your conception until the time of your death, as one long, continuous ceremony, filled with many rituals, some familiar, some unknown and challenging. Your home and all your relations, the altar. You, part of many seasons and cycles.

Now see this ceremony of your life as part of a much larger ceremony that extends seven generations into the past and seven into the future, made up of many births and deaths. This beautiful spinning earth the altar. You, part of the great ebb and flow.

Now, if you will, imagine this larger ceremony to be but one part of a ceremony so grand and magnificent as to be hardly comprehensible, a great, vast ceremonial circle, rich and vibrant with millions upon millions of swirling circles of dancing light, and you, one of those dancing circles, a dancer on the altar that is the Universe, where time is eternal.

May You Dance in Beauty

CIRCLE = disk,
round, roundlet, roundel,
wheel, ring, band, hoop, cordon,
annulus, crown, coronet, diadem, halo,
corona, aureole, wreath, garland, belt, cinc-
ture, girth, bracelet , circlet, arena, rink, cir-
cus, orb , ball, globe, realm, sphere, dominion,
circumference, perimeter, periphery, radius,
compass, scope, extent, zone, theater, bounds,
neighborhood, group, set, coterie, knot, ring,
crowd, club, society, association, cycle,
circuit, full turn, twirl, gyration, spiral, ron-
dure, coil, whorl, vortex, rotate, revolve, whirl,
twirl, reel, turn, spin, orbit, circumnavigate,
ensphere, encompass, envelop, embrace,
pirouette, pivot, loop, coil, circum-
rotate, circumvolve, circulate,
= REVOLUTION

APPENDIX

For books of circle songs write:

Circle Song Book by Yaffa Rosenthal, Box 574, Trinidad, CA 95570

Songs of the Earth by Anna Kealola, c/o Celestial Arts, P.O. Box 7327, Berkeley, CA 94707

To buy handmade gourd rattles painted with your totems or symbols write:

Jana Holmer, Starfish Designs, P.O. Box 2151, Big Bear City, CA 92314

To order handmade drums write:

Alexandra Hart (deerskin, handpainted), P.O. Box 1938, Sebastopol, CA 95472

Chester Bear Eagle (native drums), Box 34, Miwok Village, CA 95346

David Pierce, 1948 Citrus Ave., Chico, CA 94926

Golden Eagle Drum Co. (excellent dumbeks), c/o Larry Mitchell, 1641 Somerset Ave., Cardiff, CA 92007

Arthur Hull (congas), Village Music Circles, 108 Coalinga Way, Santa Cruz, CA 95060

Carraway (congas & others), Box 1483, San Rafael, CA 94912

David Schiffman, Flying Horse Ranch, Palo Colorado Canyon, Carmel, CA 93923

Gordy Ryan, 2109 Broadway, Apt. 477, New York, NY 10023

For drums, smudge, and other supplies write:

Harmony & Bear, Box 1614, San Andreas, CA 95249

Gaia Book Store, 1537 Spruce, Berkeley, CA 94709

For tapes of circle songs write:

Medicine Song Productions, Rashani, 2015 Menalto, Menlo Park, CA 94025

Dolphinsong, Unltd., Alicia Bonnet, P.O. Box 1403, Mt. Shasta, CA 96067

Artemis College, Midwife Chants, 13140 Frati Lane, Sebastopol, CA 95472

Reclaiming Chants, P.O. Box 14404, San Francisco, CA 94114

Acoustic Medicine, Nancy Goddard, 2462 Matilija Canyon, Ojai, CA 93023

Harmony Network, Brooke Medicine Eagle, P.O. Box 2550, Guerneville, CA 95446

For tapes about circles & vision questing write:

New Dimensions Tapes, P.O. Box 410510, San Francisco, CA 94141
(A one-hour tape recording of Sedonia & Bird talking about The Vision Quest is available.)

Jeanne Paslé-Green, KPFA, P.O. Box 13011, Berkeley, CA 94704
(A one-hour tape recording of the Owl/Eagle Lodge talking about their lodge, drumming, and singing, and a one-hour tape recording of Sedonia & Bird talking about Restoring the Sacred Hoop, including storytelling and music are available.)

For information about vision questing, teaching, and workshops write:

Sedonia Cahill & Bird Brother, The Great Round, P.O. Box 1772, Sebastopol, CA 95473

For information about Rainbow Drumming Circle Process work write:

Joshua Halpern, c/o The Essential Oneness Healing Alliance (TEO-HA), Box 5, Bodega, CA 94922

To order a quarterly newsletter about circles write:

Earth Circle News, P.O. Box 1938, Sebastopol, CA 95473

Sedonia Cahill has a master of arts in psychology with an emphasis on self-generated ritual. She is a vision quest guide, teacher, and ceremonialist and has a private counseling practice. She is the cofounder of The Great Round, a nonprofit organization dedicated to the promotion of the circle.

Joshua Halpern is a writer and drummer who has also, in turn, been a vegetarian chef, naturopathic doctor, and apprenticed midwife. He has a master's degree in community psychology. His previous works include *Live Your Health* and *Children of the Dawn*.

3-4-96, VRomans, 15(12), 63025